Contents

How to Use this Book

This book contains references to videos which accompany the text. While of course, it is impossible to view a video in a paper book, there are various options as to how they can be accessed.

The easiest option is that in each section where a video is mentioned, there will be a square black and white QR code pictured below. To use these you will need to download a QR scanner app onto your phone or tablet. Once you have undertaken this whenever you see a similar code, you can scan it, to be taken directly to the correct Youtube link.

Should you need to view the videos on a computer, they can be accessed via the website: www.plasticheroes.co.uk and following the link to the book resources page. You may wish to download them from Youtube for viewing offline.

If neither of these approaches is successful for you, you can contact me and request a copy of the videos. My email contact details are included at the end of the book.

Chapter 1 - Foreword.

Note on terminology: Within this book, there will be discussion and explanation of universal climbing techniques. I may use words such as "route", "climb", "bloc" or "boulder". Equally photos of both bouldering and roped climbs are used. The techniques described are equally applicable to boulder problems or roped routes, so whatever terminology is used, apply the techniques to the type of climbing you prefer.

By purchasing this book, you have taken the first step to gaining perfect technique. This could be because you are new to climbing and want to set off on the right foot. Equally, you could have plateaued and can't find the best way to break through and make more progress. You may also be coaching yourself, or other climbers. This book illustrates how to climb efficiently and outlines the most effective techniques to get you climbing closest to your potential. Each section has photos and videos demonstrating how to undertake the skills effectively. This will provide you with a model to copy in your own climbing and many of the sections include effective ways of coaching and explaining the skills to other climbers. It is designed to be read in stages with the training plan following each section, which will cement the techniques into your climbing.

Coaching sections are provided at the end of each topic. These are in the red printed boxes. This book is not just designed for self improvement, also for coaching friends, children or classes. This book is designed to follow the BMC Fundamentals courses and the Mountain Training Coaching qualifications. It provides indicators of when the techniques are undertaken correctly and when more improvement is required.

The techniques will take time to perfect, and you need to expect your performance to dip slightly whilst your technique evolves. It is natural to want to abandon something which feels hard and sometimes un-natural, however if seen through to the end, overall you will be climbing more efficiently than when you started. It is the same in many sports when new techniques are learned or changes are made. Performance dips until the new technique is practised and integrated, however once this occurs you will be climbing much better in the end. The training plan at the end of this book will take a minimum of 36 weeks to complete. This is without the repetition of any sections or taking any breaks to consolidate the new techniques into your climbing style. You should expect that your performance will see a gradual improvement while your skill level raises, rather than being a quick fix.

While the basics covered in Set 1 may seem ... basic, it is important to complete each section before moving onto the next. Technique and the training plan can be broken down into manageable stages and dedicating time to increase your proficiency of each of the sections will improve your overall technique level and climbing ability.

When self-analysing and attempting to determine what aspect to work on, we frequently can't see the wood from the trees. With the technique plan at the end, you will be guided in improving a range of important areas. Once this is completed, you should be able to identify and isolate specific areas of improvement, and repeat sections as necessary.

The first problem with identifying that we need technique development, is that climbs at our limit - either boulder problems or routes, feel physically hard. This makes us feel that we are not strong enough to complete the route, and the obvious solution is to put on muscle. My philosophy is: develop technique rather than physique. Personally, I am incredibly lazy and lifting weights or continual endurance climbing seems like hard work compared to training efficiency. That isn't to say that strong people necessarily have poor technique. But the more someone is able to "pull" through a move, the less likely they are to devote time to technique. Getting accustomed to pulling makes the techniques harder to learn as they feel more and more alien, the more dependent on pulling the climber becomes. The best climbers in the world are very strong, but also climb with grace and technical efficiency. Strength does have its role within climbing and it cannot be denied that climbing significantly harder requires more strength. However, I consider that the majority of climbers who climb twice or more per week, already have sufficient strength to climb their projects and harder. What would be of benefit is training technique to improve their grade. However, many people hit the training room or undertake endurance programmes instead. This book is based on the premise that technical efficiency should be mastered before undertaking endurance or power training.

Why Climb With Technique When I Can Get Stronger?

In a nutshell, it boils down to efficiency verses power. Any car enthusiast will already have made a decision about what they prefer: generally ... Power (myself included)! However there are a number of reasons why as climbers we should devote our time to improving technical efficiencies rather than training to be stronger and equipping ourselves with a larger engine.

More Aesthetic, Efficient Climbing Style.

Think of a lift, gliding up between floors in a smooth movement. Take a second to make a mental picture of this lift. What does it look like? What type of building is it in?

Now think of a lift which is jerking up and down, still moving between the similar floors but in a jerky up and down fashion. Again, make a mental image of this lift. What does this one look like? What type of building is this one in?

Which one is more efficient? Which one would you prefer to get into? We might not know what is wrong with the jerky lift, however we think something is amiss and would probably avoid it.

The majority of people picture the first lift being plush and posh, in either an expensive hotel or modern office block. For the second lift people generally visualise a lift in a rundown block of flats or a dirty hotel which is badly lit and dingy.

Watch climbers with good technique, their climbing looks effortless. This is because we are trained to associate graceful movements with appeal. This has little to do with the strength of the climber. Similarly when we look at something which is not efficient, it looks hard work. Visualise climbers jerking up and down. Every. Time. They. Grab. For. A. Hold. Climbing with strength as opposed to technique is likely to result in this jerky, plainly inefficient movement. This book will give you the tricks and tips to climb with efficiency.

Advantages of Technique over Strength.

Get Less Tired Allowing for Longer or Harder Climbing Sessions.

Efficiency = greater performance for the same energy. A basic concept, but one which we forget as soon as we get on the wall. Performance means different things to different people. Some people consider harder climbs as increased performance. Others consider climbing an increased number of times while keeping the grade the same to be higher performance. Whatever your definition of greater performance, increasing your efficiency will enable you to climb longer and / or harder before your forearms are tired, your grip fails and your session is over.

Returning to Climbing.

Sometimes life gets in the way. We have all had time off climbing. This could be weeks, months or even years. Unless we are undertaking climbing specific training during our time off, we are going to lose much of our physical climbing strength and our performance is bound to drop. If our main climbing attribute is strength, the performance and level of our climbing will drop significantly. If we have developed perfect technique prior to our time off, while these skills may be a little rusty, our performance drop is less. It takes much less time and effort to retrain our technique to return to our previous standard. It just like riding a bike! Even if climbing sporadically we can maintain a reasonable standard close to our potential. For the past 18 months, I have only been able to climb a maximum of couple of times per week for roughly 30 minutes to an hour per session. Blame the baby! However my current climbing is still within a couple of grades of my previous performance. This is due to technique.

Injury Avoidance.

For the two reasons listed in the paragraphs above, greater efficiency would benefit the majority of climbers as opposed to strength. Returning to the car analogy, an inefficient climber is like driving a car with the brakes partially on. Regardless of the power or size of the engine it will never be as efficient as it could be, and the top speed (hardest route) or the economy (endurance / length of climbing session) will never be as good as a comparable but efficient model. Also consider that more fuel is required to power an inefficient car and parts wear out faster. So an inefficient climber needs to train strength more than an efficient climber to undertake the same climbs.

Looking at recent literature relating to injuries and injury avoidance, none mention preventing injuries when developing technique. I consider that developing efficient technique is a vastly safer way of improving your climbing with significantly less chance of injury.

Agreement.

Before reading further about technique development, there are some agreements which you should consider prior to undertaking the improvement plan.

1. I agree to the participation statement below and will exercise reasonable precautions when undertaking the training plan to avoid accident or injury.
2. Until the improvement plan has been completed, I will not undertake strength training.
3. I will climb twice a week as a minimum (three times is optimal).
4. I will undertake this plan with a regular climbing partner.

Participation Statement.

It is universally accepted that climbing is an activity with a danger of injury or death. By reading this book and practicing the techniques contained therein, you should accept these risks and be responsible for your own actions. You should be competent to exercise all reasonable precautions to remain safe while climbing and undertaking the technical improvement exercises. This should include, but not be limited to:

- Knowing your own capabilities and climbing within them.
- Taking reasonable precautions on bouldering problems.
- Having a suitable level of familiarity with top rope safety: fitting a harness, tying in and belaying.
- Being proficient at lead climbing, belaying and knowing the additional risks associated with this climbing discipline.
- Having a reasonable knowledge of climbing injuries and injury avoidance.

No Strength Training.

Technique and strength are completely separate. There are times where they conflict, especially on harder routes. There are times where strength will feel easier until the technique is fully learned and proficient. The technical improvement will provide you with more tools with which to efficiently complete climbs. Once they are learned, you will need to decide on the most efficient way to complete a climb. However continuing to train strength while trying to improve technique will have a detrimental impact. The training plan will not be as effective, and it will take much longer to complete.

Climbing Twice Per Week.

Climbing a minimum of twice a week is imperative to the training plan working. If you are only able to climb for one session a week, the amount of time that will be devoted to technical improvement will be limited given the urge to climb challenging routes. The precise nature of the training plans mean that if undertaken in isolation with no rewarding climbing, it is likely to prove de-motivating leading to your climbing being un-enjoyable. People often try and split climbing sessions and focus one half on technique and the other half on climbing hard routes. Try not to do this! Swapping mid session is much less effective than two distinct sessions. It is difficult for the brain to switch from training to performance climbing without continuing to analyse technique. Even if you complete hard routes which you are happy about, you are still likely to be critical that there were times when your technique could have been improved, reducing the sense of achievement. What is much better is to undertake the training plan, and if you still have time and energy to climb, undertake fun climbing with your partner and resist the urge to consider or comment upon each other's climbing style.

When I was devoting time to my technique, I climbed three times a week. One session was for working on the plan and improving technically. The second session was working project routes or boulders. The third session was: can you make your climber laugh so hard they are unable to climb and fall off. The combination of three distinct sessions kept me motivated and resulted in me improving technically, seeing the results, progressing on problems, and let's not forget why we started climbing. To have fun!

Having a Regular, Supportive Climbing Partner.

Choosing the correct person with whom to undertake your training will be the most important decision you will make aside from deciding to implement this plan. As well as keeping you safe, they will also be your guide and coach.

When we climb it is impossible to see how we are moving. Even if we video ourselves (which can be useful for feedback) we do not get real time direction or corrections about our technique. Often what feels right is actually wrong and vice versa. You need someone to tell you about your technique while you are climbing. For example, during a climb your arms feel really tired. Naturally you might consider you are too weak for the climb and need to get stronger to complete it. Your climbing partner however can see that your arms are bent and your balance is off, correctly identifying that you don't need more strength. Rather, improving balance and dropping down onto straight arms will make the climb more efficient and feel easier.

It is helpful if your climbing partner undertakes the improvement plan alongside you, so that you can encourage, motivate and train each other to perfect these techniques, while both getting something out of the sessions.

What makes a good training partner:

- Keeping you safe.
- Agreeing with your training plan.
- Being attentive to your technique and required improvement.
- Providing you with real time feedback.
- Committing to train with you at least once a week to work on the techniques together.

Chapter 2 - The Techniques.

This book is not intended to be read in one go. You should dip in and out of the relevant sections depending on the techniques you are training. The book is split into sets as detailed below.

Training Set	Focuses on
Set 1 / Chapter 3: The Fundamentals.	<ul><li>Footwork & precise placements.</li><li>Balance and rocking over.</li><li>Handholds and the direction of pull - Basic Route Reading.</li><li>Straight arms.</li></ul>
Set 2 / Chapter 4: Twisting.	Twisting - <ul><li>Outside Edge.</li><li>Flagging.</li></ul>
Set 3 / Chapter 5: Twisting Refined.	Techniques - <ul><li>Pivoting.</li><li>Drop knees.</li><li>Exaggerated Twisting.</li><li>Bridging and Planting.</li><li>Starting Boulder Problems.</li><li>Heel and Toe Hooks.</li><li>Dynamic Moves.</li></ul> Skills - <ul><li>Route Reading.</li><li>Appropriate twisting.</li><li>Finding and use of rests.</li><li>Appropriate clipping position.</li><li>Appropriate use of speed on a climb.</li><li>Controlling Fear and Falling.</li></ul>
Set 4 / Chapter 6: Plateauing	<ul><li>Evaluating and targeting further training needs.</li></ul>
Chapter 7: The Training Plan	

Sets and Exercises Explained.

Each set detailed above is progressive. The skills and techniques learned in each set underpin the skills to be learned in the next stage of the training plan. Avoid trying to read the whole book and attempting to skip straight to the more advanced techniques. Building a good understanding of the basics is of much more use and will ensure that you progress better and faster as a result.

Set 1 focuses on the fundamentals underpinning all climbing movement. By the time it is completed, you will have the skills to climb any route on a slab and vertical walls should be much easier. It may be that your skills will need to be refined to climb the hardest slab routes, but the understanding of the principles behind how to climb them will have been learned.

Set 2 focuses on learning to change your centre of gravity. It will allow more effective pushing by the legs on primarily overhanging, but also vertical walls. While this is the shortest chapter in the book, it is the most important to learn correctly when climbing overhanging walls. A significant amount of time has been allocated for this section in the training plan to ensure the techniques are correctly learned.

Set 3 refines the skills learned in set 2. Introduces more techniques for climbing overhanging routes and starts to focus more on tactics to enable you to determine which style to use to effectively climb a route.

Set 4 provides tips on analysing your climbing so that you are able to determine what further improvements can be made. This should be able to help you when you plateau.

Once a set is completed, you can either repeat the set, following the training plan as before or by repeating specific sections which require greater attention. You can always dip out of the plan, taking time to integrate the skills effectively into your climbing repertoire before moving on. Or you could move straight onto the next set.

Once you have completed all the sets, and refined your technique until it is perfect, it may be time to consider strength training. Keep revisiting your technique. Ensure that you are still climbing in the most efficient way possible and that the strength training complements your technical efficiency.

Before continuing further, you need to decide which set to begin with. Many people should start from Set 1. The techniques in Set 1 underpin all of the subsequent learning and you should have a good grounding in these prior to progressing. Whichever Set you decide to begin with, read that whole chapter, then start the training plan for that section. When commencing the first week, the relevant section should be read again, and the exercises practised. After that, follow the rest of the plan until the end of the allocated weeks. Have a week's rest from the plan, then move onto the next section.

Chapter 3 - Set 1: The Fundamentals.

The three fundamentals of good climbing technique are **Precise Footwork, Good Balance and Straight Arms.** These are interlinked. If you have good balance and straight arms, this will enable your footwork to be precise and not rushed. This leads to a solid foundation for your legs to efficiently push you up the climb. If all three fundamentals are used effectively, you will progress smoothly up the wall. If either balance or straight arms deteriorate, foot placements are likely to become rushed and inaccurate leading to a poor foundation. More weight will be transferred onto your arms. This gets tiring very quickly. The following training teaches how to climb more efficiently utilising these fundamentals.

Precise Footwork.

Learning to place your feet on the holds perfectly, first time, every time, without changing or testing them is a skill that cannot be underestimated. It gets harder on smaller holds, but is even more important to place your feet correctly. Precise footwork builds a strong, trusted foundation enabling effective pushing with the feet.

When beginners or improvers climb, it can be noticeable that their footwork needs to be improved to progress onto harder climbs. It may look and sound a little sloppy with much scuffing and banging. When footwork needs improvement, it feels like the arms are taking a lot of weight, so people often have the misconception that they are not strong enough to climb harder.

Video 1 shows the common problems with climbers footwork from beginners to more advanced climbers. There are three main problems which occur in climbers footwork:

- Incorrect position or part of the foot in contact with the hold.
- Not looking at the foot holds.
- Testing (ankle bounce) or repositioning the foot by feel.

Position of the foot.

While there are many ways we can place our feet onto holds, in this section, we will focus on the Inside Edge. The inside edge, is quite simply put, the inside edge of your foot. It runs from the big toe, down to the heel. Leaving the heel to be considered later, the inside edge can be split into four areas; see the photo below. Which part of the foot would you feel most confident using?

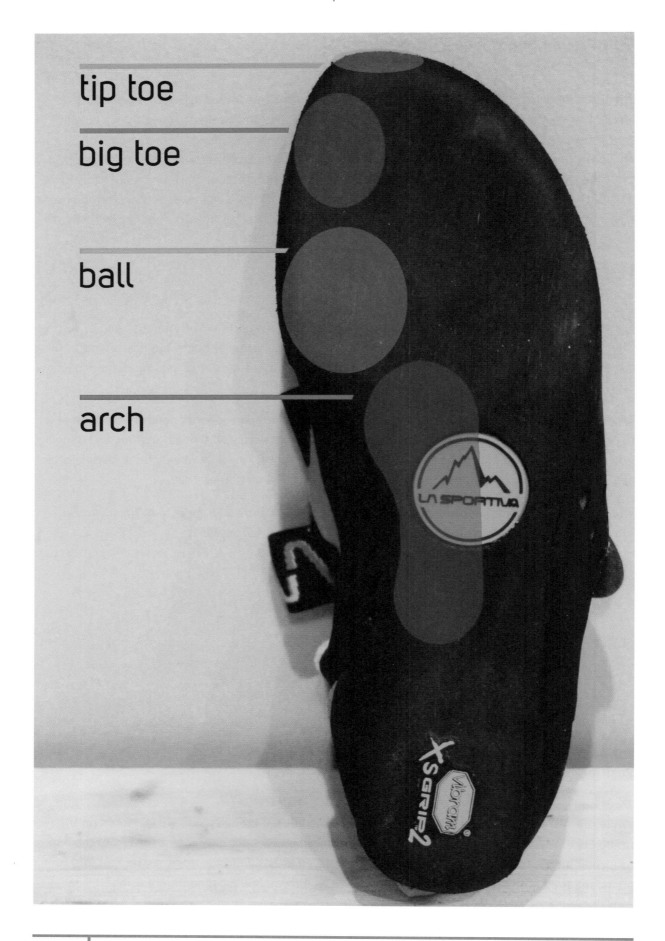

tip toe

big toe

ball

arch

The default position for the inside edge should be the big toe. Utilizing the big toe has two main advantages, firstly it is the most precise area of the foot to place onto the hold. Secondly, it is able to feel much more. Try pointing your toes and pressing the inside of your big toe into the floor. How much are you able to feel? Repeat with the ball of the foot. You should be able to feel much more with the big toe which will lead to a more precise foot placement and more confidence using the hold.

The tip of the toes, like ballerinas on point, should be placed into pockets or holes in the wall **if** this will result in a better contact. Consider the amount of surface area between shoe and hold. If tip toes have more contact and will create a more stable platform, use the toes. See the photos below for differing options.

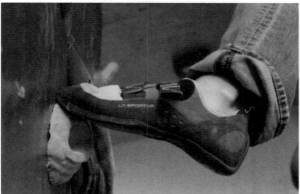 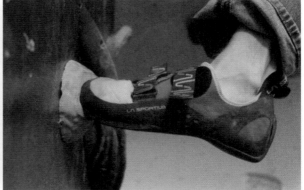

Beginners tend to place their feet too far forward on the holds. When looking at beginners footwork, you are likely to notice the toes being over the edge of the hold. This leads to the ball of the foot or even worse the arch being used to stand up on the holds. The ball of the foot is less precise than the big toe as detailed above. The arch does nothing positive and should be avoided at all costs. There is little reason as to why beginners use the arch, as to experienced climbers, it feels very unstable, and has the following disadvantages with no benefits.

Reducing Hold Size.

As the pictures below demonstrate, when a shoe is placed square against a wall, there is a large gap created where the shoe bends in at the arch. This reduces the size of any foothold. On larger holds, this may not be a particular issue, however when progressing, the reduction in hold size can be drastic enough to stop us from gaining any meaningful purchase. On even smaller holds, the shoe can fit right past the hold without even coming into contact with it.

 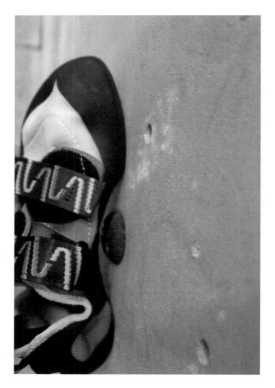

On the Arch; Every Hold is a Sloper.

Turn over a new pair of climbing shoes and look at the soles. The edges around the toe invariably have a 90° edge on the rubber. This allows a great, precise contact between shoe and hold. As shoes get more and more worn, they become rounded, to the point that they are not trusted and either are resoled or put in the bin. Now look at the arch. Generally, there is no identified edge, and if the arch comes in contact with a hold, the effect is that the slope around the arch gets little purchase on the hold. This will feel very tenuous and is unlikely to encourage pushing with the feet.

Greater Height with the Toe.

Put very simply, using the heel or the arch of the foot results in an inability to stand on tip toes. On some routes, this can make the difference between whether or not the next handhold can be reached.

Not Looking at the Holds.

Not looking at footholds is one of the main reasons why beginners footwork is poor. Aside from a glance down at the feet to see where the holds are, how much do we actually look at the feet as opposed to looking up at the hands? An easy way to test this is to climb with a small camera mounted on your head. As discussed before, if feet are the foundation to our climbing, we should pay as much attention to them as possible to ensure that they provide a strong, stable base. Check your video. Are you looking at your feet? Are you really looking at every foothold until you have weighted it? If you just see your hands grabbing for holds, it is time to improve your footwork.

In addition to paying too much attention to their hands, people tend to look away a second or so before they place their feet onto the holds. This is similar to taking aim, then looking away a second or so before firing. Aim and precision are likely to be well off. Keep looking until the foot is in contact with the hold!

The last error which also counts as not looking at the hold is when the foot is kicked onto the wall above and then slid / scraped down the wall until it is on the hold. For the obvious reason that you cannot see through your foot, you lose sight of the foothold and therefore any precision. Also and from a financial point, you will replace your shoes very frequently as the rubber will wear out in no time at all. (I shouldn't say this really, owning a shop and all!)

Testing Footholds.

Testing footholds is pointless and very energy intensive. Again, look at beginners and climbers using smaller footholds. It is likely that even on reasonably large footholds there is a distinct ankle bounce, and probably a few, before the climber commits to putting weight on to the foot hold. Often the climber also repositions the foot a number of times, testing each placement. How long does someone test for? Normally it is only a couple of seconds per hold, however all this time adds up to quite a considerable amount over the course of a climb. If the foot holds are smaller, the time spent testing can be greatly increased and I have seen people testing footholds for up to a minute before having to use them anyway.

When we are testing, we *may* be balanced, we *may* have straight arms, but in most cases it is likely that we will not. This leads to wasting time testing holds, while being in a very strenuous position which overall is very tiring. In short, if you see ankle bounce testing or frequent repositioning of the foot, tell the climber to stop testing. They should remove and carefully replace their foot and commit to using the foot hold. Testing is just as important in bouldering as climbing routes, because while there are less moves, it is likely that your position and orientation on the wall is likely to be far more strenuous. Even if you are moving onto, and can climb the harder routes, foot testing as demonstrated in the initial video, makes the climb much harder than it needs to be. Improving footwork makes the climb smoother, more efficient and ultimately less strength is required to undertake it.

Perfecting Foot Placements.

Now that we know which part of the foot to use and the errors to avoid, we can concentrate on how to place the foot on the holds in the best possible way. The following five steps will take time and practise to learn, however will greatly improve your climbing in the long run.

The 5 Steps of Good Footwork:

1. Look at the foothold... continue to look until step 4 has been completed.
2. Place your foot close to the foothold.
3. Determine the angle of the hold and match the angle of your foot with the angle of the hold.
4. Place your foot onto the hold. No changes or ankle bounce tests. If there are repositions or tests, remove your foot and repeat stages 1-4.
5. Transfer your weight onto the foothold and stand.

Once you have learned to undertake this technique, you will be getting much more out of your foot work. You should be maximising the surface area between your foot and the hold. This enables you to trust your foot and provides a stable platform to push from. Continue to practise footwork until it is completely proficient and you no longer have to think about the five steps when placing your foot to get a perfect contact. Once you are able to do this, you have learned to climb with good footwork.

Note: when the holds slant upwards, they feel reasonably secure, even when they are quite small. When the holds slant down (away from us), we need to point the toe down. This feels quite insecure, even on quite large, positive holds. To make them feel more secure, imagine pulling the hold towards you with the toe, just like you would if pulling a coin towards you on the floor. Keep pulling, until your centre of gravity is over the foothold and your weight is pushing directly down onto the hold. It should feel much more secure when your weight is directly over the foot.

Exercise: Practicing the 5 Steps.

Practise climbing easy routes with perfect footwork. At first you should go through the 5 steps every time you place your foot onto a hold. This will be a slow process and to start off with, climbs will take longer to accomplish. However like learning any skill, slow down to gain perfection, then speed up as your skill increases. Think of learning a new piece of music. It is practised slowly until correct before being played at full speed. Learning these skills should be no different. Taking this time to learn the placement skills correctly will result in them becoming automatic, more precise and faster later on. Your footwork should be silent, with perfect placements and no testing or repositioning of your foot. Once you have perfected footwork on larger holds, practise on slowly smaller and less positive ones. To avoid injury when using smaller footholds, keep your hands on large, positive holds so you are able to concentrate on your footwork without too much weight being placed onto your hands.

Video 2 shows the improved footwork of the volunteers from their original climb.

Video 3 demonstrates optimum footwork to aim for. The footwork is not rushed, always leading to a good foot placement with maximum contact between the foot and the hold. The climber looks at the foot hold until the foot is placed. Once the foot is placed onto the hold, there is no testing. Instead, the climber transfers their weight over their foot, and stands.

Coaching:

When looking to correct footwork, the climber needs to slow down. The faster they climb, the more difficult it is to place their feet correctly. It is also harder for you to spot and correct any errors. It is also difficult for the climber to remember the error a couple of moves ago after you have made them aware something needed correction.

While undertaking the exercises, footwork should be silent (or as close to it as possible). The climber should be visually going through the 5 steps each time they place their foot.
Once their foot is placed onto the hold, it should not be repositioned. If the foot is moved, have the climber remove the foot from the hold and go through the first few steps again.

If the climber tests the hold with the ankle bounce, have them remove the foot, replace it more carefully, then rock over the foot hold.

Once footwork has improved on easy climbs and holds, have the climber keep the same handholds, but use smaller footholds on a differing route. If there are no small holds, they can only use the corners of larger holds to reduce the size in contact with the foot. When the size of holds reduces, expect to see an increase in the amount of testing undertaken. Ensure the climber goes through the 5 stages and then rocks straight over rather than undertaking the ankle bounce test. The more ankle bounce testing that is undertaken, the more it will be relied upon and the harder it will be to get out of this habit.

A great number of coaches use corks to reduce the size of large foot holds. I advocate a better approach is for the climber to keep their hands on the same large holds, but to just use smaller footholds. The reasons for this are as follows:

- When undertaking climbing with corks, participants are very careful about getting the foot as close to the cork as possible without touching it. However less attention is made to the actual placement of their foot onto the hold. The value of placing the foot precisely onto the hold is overshadowed by concentrating on not touching or knocking over the cork.
- Climbers will spend much longer on a climb avoiding the corks rather than using smaller footholds. As climbers spend much longer on the climb than is necessary, this extra time is spent hanging off the arms. This makes good footwork seem physically hard. The benefits of precise foot placements are therefore overshadowed by the strenuous nature of the exercise. What we should coach is precise but efficiently speedy foot placements.
- If the cork is placed on the near side of the hold, the foot is unlikely to be able to be placed onto the hold in an effective inside edge position. The foot is forced perpendicular to the wall and the tip toes are used rather than an effective inside edge. The issue with this is covered above.

It is more beneficial to think of a positive rather than a negative. It is therefore better to look at a small hold and know you have all of that hold to stand on, rather than being told do not use certain sections of a larger hold.

Smearing.

Smearing sounds exactly like what we are doing - smearing our feet into the wall to get them to stick. Why take our feet off the holds at all? Consider the photos below. Photo 1 has a large gap between the handholds and the next foot hold. Photo 2 has a handhold, but no foothold below or further out for balance. Rather than try and place your left foot very high on the next hold which will require both strength and flexibility, smearing is likely to be a more effective solution.

Common problems with smearing involve:

- Bent arms - puts lots of weight on the arms. This is because you are pushing with your legs, and the arm muscles are pulling to keep you onto the wall. Sink onto straight arms and hang off the skeleton to avoid this strenuous position. Also your feet are unable to reach quite so high when you are in a vertical position. They will therefore slip. Leaning back and smearing pushes the feet into the wall so they will stick. It also allows the feet to walk onto higher holds.

- Low or high feet. The angle your feet are pushing into the wall determines whether they will stick or slip. The lower your feet are, the more you will be pushing down the wall rather than in and there is a greater chance that they will slip. Conversely if the feet are too high, they will push back off the hands, resulting in a very strenuous position.

The correct smearing point should be undertaken with straight arms, and feet mid-way between a high and low stance. This should be where you have a reasonable balance between grip with the feet and not placing too much weight onto the hands. Expect that as climbs change, your smearing point may also be altered. In some circumstances you may need to smear higher. For example, if the wall is polished or grip for the feet is not very good. Examples of where you may need to smear lower may be to reduce weight from the hands - if the handholds are particularly poor.

Exercise: Finding a Smearing Point.

- Using big holds for your hands, stick your bum down to the floor and hang off the handholds with straight arms.
- Step up and off the holds so your feet are between knee and waist height (if standing up normally on the previous holds.)
- Toes pointing up towards the top of the wall, the ball of the foot should be on the wall.
- This position should be similar to lowering off at the top of the climb before you let go.
- Walk your feet up the wall onto the next hold of choice. Keep the upper body in the same position.
- Once your foot is on the hold, rock your weight over the foot hold and stand.
- Pick 2 more large holds for the hands and a foothold to smear to.
- Repeat until you are at the top of the wall.

The important thing for this exercise is to determine what works for you. Each person is different and while the principle is the same, experiment to find your optimal smearing position.

Smearing Exercise Variation 1.

- Having found a suitable smear point, try raising your feet. The higher they are; the more strength is required to hold on.
- Try lowering your feet. Less strength is required, but there is a higher chance your feet will slip.
- See what happens when you bend your arms. Your feet will almost certainly slip as bending your arms means your feet are pushing more down the wall than in, and cannot gain much grip.

Smearing Exercise Variation 2.

Try smearing quickly with one foot, rocking your weight out to that side to get it to stick. This enables the other foot to quickly step up onto a hold. When rocking back, your weight rocks straight back over your foot for a stable placement. This smearing variation takes practise to get the timing right, however is required for some of the more advance climbs when a quick smear is required on poor handholds.

Video 4 demonstrates smearing in a couple of differing scenarios as described above.

Good Balance.

When climbing slabs or vertical walls, the climbers weight or centre of gravity should be between their feet or directly over one foot. Hands should be only as far apart as the feet, preferably in between. To easily gain a balanced position on a vertical wall or slab, both feet should be pointing outwards so you are using the inside edge. This will look like a crab or space invader.

So why don't we stay in this position all of the time? When we move from hold to hold, consider what do we normally look for first, is it the next hand hold or foot hold? Generally people look for the next hand hold. The reason for this is a hand hold will generally feel much more secure than a foot hold. We can grip the hand hold, give it a tug and know that the hand will remain on the hold. It makes us feel more secure.

The problem with this is if we move our hand out to the side first, the foot on that side is now bearing the majority of our weight. We therefore have to effectively do an assisted pull up to relieve enough weight from the foot so that we are able to move it to the next hold and regain a balanced position. We then again look for the next hand hold, pinning the foot we need to move and the process is repeated, doing assisted pull ups on each move on the climb. You can see in the first photo below, the climbers weight is equalised between both feet. In the second photo, their left foot bears the majority of his weight and is driven down into the matting.

You can test this at home using the very high tech equipment of a set of bathroom scales. Start with one foot on and one foot off the scales. Your feet should be just over shoulder width apart, and your hands above your feet in a square, balanced position. The same as the photo above. You should see that roughly half your body weight is through each foot. Now test moving the hand which is over the scales directly out to the side. It should move roughly 30-40 cm at the same height it previously was. This will force you to shift your centre of gravity further over the foot on the scales, the same as when we make a similar movement on the wall. You will see an increase in the weight being put on to the foot on the scales. The larger the reach to the side, the more weight is placed onto the foot and the more strenuous the move becomes. We found that a hand movement of even 30-40 cm to the side will almost double the weight on the foot and be reasonably close to your whole body weight. When we try and move that foot, the weight will have to be taken by the hands. It can be surprising just how hard we have to work when we make moves off balance compared to when we make the same moves in a well-balanced position. The comparison is demonstrated in video 5.

While this may not notice on individual, easy moves it all adds up, and is a complete waste of energy. The following three exercises reinforce that climbing with good balance is significantly easier and a much better, more efficient way of climbing.

Exercise 1: Feeling Unbalanced Climbing.

Start in a balanced position with your hands between the footholds. Both feet should be pointing out to the side like a ballet dancer or a frog. Move **either** your hands or feet off to one side keeping the other still. This should be done in small stages, noticing how much weight is transferred onto the hands as they get further outside of your feet. You should end up leaning diagonally to one side, with both hands off to one side of your feet. This will illustrate just how hard it is to climb when our hands reach outside of our feet and should be avoided.

> Coaching:
>
> When setting the exercise up, the climber should use large hand and foot holds. It is also helpful if there are a range of large handholds or footholds to move to in small increments. It is more effective for the climber to move their hands rather than their feet. As soon as both hands are to one side of their feet, a large amount of strength in their arms and core will be required to remain on the holds. It is easier if the climber moves the opposite hand to the way they are moving first. For example, if the climber is moving to the right, moving the left hand first to each position will be more achievable to get into the diagonal, off balance position. Be aware that the climber will be likely to swing off the holds when they get into an unbalanced position. Expect them to swing or fall and take reasonable precautions to prevent injury.

Exercise 2: Balanced Climbing - Traversing.

This exercise corrects the off balance position felt in exercise 1. It should be undertaken straight afterwards so you can feel the full effect of the difference. Start in the original balanced position using the same holds. Moving across an easy traverse wall, you should look like a "crab or space invader" ensuring the hands remain within the feet. If moving to the right, as a general rule, look for the next hand hold, then before moving your right hand, move your right foot to a hold below or wider than the hand hold. Now that you have a wide base, you can move your hands across to the next holds. Lastly, move your left foot below your left hand. To ensure you always remain balanced, consider moving foot, hand, hand, foot but the main priority is to ensure feet remain as wide, if not wider than your hands.

> Coaching:
>
> Ensure that the climbers feet point out so they are using the inside edge of the foot. In this position, it is very difficult to move their centre of gravity outside of their feet and therefore get off balance.
>
> Have the climber experiment with transferring their weight by pushing from side to side with their feet rather than pulling with their arms. If the climber has straight arms, when one foot pushes, it

releases weight from the other foot allowing it to be moved easily. This will of course transfer weight onto the pushing foot an-d slightly the arms, however it should be not much more strenuous than just holding a rest position because the foot is the main driver. When this is undertaken correctly, with straight arms and the legs pushing, the climber should look like they are swinging underneath each handhold, just like a monkey.

Exercise 3: Balanced Climbing - Perfecting Rock Overs.

Move on to a slab. Normally, when we climb a slab, especially an easy one, we are tempted to move diagonally, pulling with the hands as we push with the legs. If we climb like this, we will move up and across in one diagonal movement demonstrated in video 6.

The problem with this, is that without adjusting our centre of gravity to be directly over the foot, rather than pushing up, our legs push us off to the side. Two potential problems with this are: firstly, larger steps with no hand holds are not possible. The second problem is when our hands are put back on the holds, our feet push us one way and our hands have to pull us back to a balanced position. Basically all the way up the climb, we have an arm v leg wrestle. This may work on large, positive holds, albeit more a tiring way of climbing. However, if the holds are poor or are very small, it is unlikely that we will have the strength or grip with the hands to undertake the move in this way. Even routes with a modest difficulty become un-climbable. So how can we correct this?

Climb a very easy route with no hand holds. Your hands can be placed flat on the wall and used just for balance. If we lean forward against the wall, our feet push off, and away from the foot holds making even big holds feel tenuous. Try and stand as vertically as possible so the feet push directly down onto the foot holds. This will give the best foot placements. When climbing, before pushing up, we need to "rock over" the higher foot. This means that your centre of gravity - i.e. the centre of your bum should move directly over the heel of your foot. In this position, you should be able to completely support your weight on the higher foot. To test this, try to remove the lower foot from the hold. If your balance is correctly over the higher foot, this should be possible. If you are unable to remove the lower foot, this is because you are not sufficiently balanced over your higher foot.

Exaggerate the rock over and move your centre of gravity even further over the higher foot. A tip to aid the balance and achieve this is to imagine that you are a waiter and have a tray of drinks in the same hand as the higher foot. When you rock over, imagine you are leaning with the tray of drinks held out for someone to take. The further you are able to reach, the more you will aid your balance. An example of correct rocking over is contained within Video 3.

Coaching:

Lots of little moves are individually easier than one large rock over. Looking to see the correct balance point can be difficult to spot. Because we are bipeds, it may feel uncomfortable or unnatural for the climber to sufficiently rock over one foot. They may gain the correct balance point, but back off a few inches so they are not correctly balanced, then push. Try and iron out these mistakes. Indicators that the climber is balanced are:

- The climbers bum is directly over their heel.
- Look at the leg bones of the climber. They will form an arrow. If the arrow points out to the side, the climber is balanced. If the arrow points diagonally up, the climber needs to rock over further.
- Can the climber remove their lower foot without falling or getting unstable? If not, they need to rock over more.

Giving the climber encouragement is key, they will feel like they are rocking over too far when in reality they are likely to need to go further. You will need to direct them. The easiest way to do this is to just call "More left" / "More right" and when in the correct position "Stand". Each time the climber does not rock over far enough, they need to come down and repeat the move.

Many coaches make people climb while holding tennis balls. While this removes the ability to pull too hard, climbers will still try and use their hands to pull using the tennis balls to get as much purchase as possible. Getting climbers used to fully rocking over and only using hands for balance (the tray of drinks example) is much more useful to developing this skill properly.

Once correct rocking over has been achieved without using your hands, re- climb the same route as before. This time replace your hands gently on to the holds. You should be concentrating on rocking over to the same position as you were reaching in "hands free" climbing. This will ensure that while your hands are replaced onto the holds you do not use them to pull and the main push up the wall still comes from the feet and legs. Expect that just using your hands for balance will feel very strange and just resting them onto the holds feels unnerving at first. Continue rocking over the feet and push while resisting the temptation to pull!

Coaching:

The indicators as to whether the climber is balanced remain the same. Be strict. When the climber puts their hands back on the holds, they will be very tempted to revert to pulling. If they do so, make them come down and redo the move with no hands. When completed with correct balance, they need to come down and redo the move a third time with the hands back on the holds. This ensures they perform the move with correct balance rather than pulling.

Straight Arms.

Keeping your arms straight on vertical and overhanging walls is the easiest way to conserve energy. This is because your skeleton takes the majority of your weight and the arm muscles are only used to keep you holding onto the wall while your legs push you up. In this section you will learn how to lean off your arms to keep them as straight and your movements as efficient as possible. Before undertaking the exercises associated with straight arms, also read and consider the next sections - Handholds and the Direction of Pull. These sections will introduce the way in which you should lean to make use of the handholds and straight arms in the easiest possible way.

Feel the difference between hanging off the wall with bent, and then straight arms. To undertake this, pick a vertical or slightly overhanging wall.

Exercise: Bent Arm Hangs.

- Find a good hold for each hand.
- Place your feet so you are balanced and comfortable.
- Pull in so you have a 90° bend in the elbow. Your face should be roughly in line with the hand holds and 30-40CM away. This will force your elbow to bend.
- If you want to exaggerate the exercise, remove one hand.
- See how long you can hold on.

Exercise: Straight Arm Hang - Comparison.

- Using the same hand and foot holds, sink down onto straight arms and feel the difference.
- With straight arms, your bottom should be hanging down to the floor, not leaning out away from the wall.
- This should feel much easier. Especially with one hand.

You can also try moving in these styles. Try a traverse (sideways climb close to the floor). Climb the route twice. First time keep the 90° bend in your arms. In this style, every time you remove a hand to move it to the next hold, pause for a second or two. This should exaggerate the amount of weight you can feel on your arms.

Return to the start and climb a second time hanging down off completely straight arms. Again, pause for a second or two mid move with only one hand holding on. The two styles should have felt drastically different. Which one felt easier? Video 7 illustrates the differences.

Coaching:

An effective drill is to tell the climber when to freeze. When the climber makes a move with a bent arm, as soon as one hand is released, tell them to freeze. Ensure the position is held for 5 seconds and that the climber remains in the bent arm position with only one hand on the wall. It will soon feel tiring and will teach them to not make moves in this manner. It is natural to feel that this is hard and the climber will try to sink down into the straight arm rest position. For them to get the benefit, ensure that they remain in the bent arm position so it feels as hard as possible.

Exercise: Climbing Up.

Climb a vertical wall ensuring that the arms are kept straight. Tip, while standing on the floor, place your hands onto the holds first. Once your hands are on the holds, sink your centre of gravity (bum) down towards the floor until your arms are straight before placing your feet on to the holds. This will provide you with the correct straight arm feeling which you can continue for the rest of the climb. If you start with bent arms and pulling as soon as you lift off the floor, it is much more likely you will continue in this style throughout the climb. Continue pushing with the feet, swinging from hold to hold keeping the arms straight.

On harder walls, it may not be possible to climb the whole route with completely straight arms. However keeping the arms straight should be used where possible to put as little strain on the muscles throughout the climb. This is especially important when shifting your weight and setting up for the next move. As demonstrated in video 8, each move the arms need to bend. They are straight however once placed onto the holds, and remain straight while the feet move to the next placements and the centre of gravity is brought into an effective position to make the next move.

Coaching:

Ensure that the climber is hanging down off straight arms. Commonly people have a tendency to lean out away from the wall with straight arms and legs as opposed to using straight arms and bent legs. This results in the grip from the hands not being in the optimal position and more strength being required to hold on. The climbers centre of gravity should pendulum from hold to hold, arcing below each hold as demonstrated below.

When traversing it is easy to adjust their position by pulling them in to the correct position. When ascending a route, rather than swinging under each hold, the climber should swing side to side keeping the arms straight until the higher hand reaches the next hold. When correct, the centre of gravity is unlikely to ascent straight up. Rather, swaying side to side as it rises, like a feather falling upwards as the photo below demonstrates.

This will mean that the arms are straight all the time and the legs are providing the drive. Classic mistakes are the climber's centre of gravity vertically ascending the route. This is likely to mean that the arms are pulling to keep the climber vertical. Video 9 illustrates this.

Note, if the climber is balanced and on a straight higher arm, the lower arm is unlikely to have much if any weight on it and may be bent. Ways of testing the amount of weight on the lower arm is for the climber to let go with their lower hand without first adjusting their centre of gravity. If they swing, have them adjust their balance point, so they take note of the correct straight arm position.

Problems.

Whether climbing or coaching, it is important to understand why we feel something. If a skill is introduced with no explanation as of why it works, it is more likely to be dismissed. The following reasons are why it can be hard to learn to climb with straight arms.

Bent Arms Feel Right.

If climbing with bent arms feels natural, and straight arms feels strange, well done, you are an evolved human being! We stand on straight legs all day, bending our arms to pick and carry things and to utilise tools. It therefore feels natural to get on the wall and climb, standing up fully on each hold using our arms to suit our legs. However to climb efficiently, we should imitate our cousins and climb like monkeys, swinging from hold to hold with arms straight in between. Looking at the initial exercise, if we use bent arms, we put ourselves in a very strenuous position. Using bent arms; muscles in the forearm, bicep and shoulder are engaged and working hard, just to keep us on to the wall. By dropping down on to straight arms, our skeleton takes the majority of the weight, removing it from the muscles. As we know, strenuous working muscles will limit us and as soon as they are too tired to use, our climbing session is over.

Straight Arms Feels Scary.

Straight arms can feel especially scary to people who have not yet gained confidence. This is because being on the wall with legs straight and arms bent, it feels like if you fall, you will be able to land on your feet. This feels quite natural and safe. On the other hand, if you are hanging down with straight arms with your bottom to the floor, if you fall off, it feels like you will land on your bum or flat on your back. Not quite as safe a feeling! While this is true, and hanging down with straight arms does risk a more serious fall, in which position are you more likely to get more tired? In which position are you more likely to fall off? You have a much higher chance of falling if you get too tired using bent arms, rather than a lower chance of falling if you use straight arms as all that energy is conserved. When you are bouldering, you will be in charge of determining which move is safe and which move feels too scary. When you are climbing with ropes, your belayer will stop you from hitting the floor, so cast out that nagging doubt and focus on climbing with your arms as straight as possible.

Forearms Feel Tired.

Some people feel that straight arms makes their forearms feel more tired. This may be true to begin with, however hanging down is much more efficient in the long run. I have found from coaching a large number of climbers, that after climbing for a month or two, you will have built up much of the climbing strength you need, until you are limited by your technique.

Once these three skills have been mastered, the climber should be able to "technically" climb any route on the slab. The only thing to improve is the exaggeration of the rock over on bigger moves, the precision of the footwork on smaller holds and the ability to smear (if required) using smaller hand holds.

Handholds.

Using handholds appears to be the most basic concept, grab a hold and pull. However devotion to using the handholds in the most effective way is key to saving forearm (grip) strength. First we will take an overview of the differing basic handholds and how they can be used the most effectively.

Jugs.

Jugs are the most favoured and easiest to use holds. The name originates from large milk jugs, which like the holds, have a large lip on top and a hole at the back for the fingers to go into. With the fingers bent over like a half clenched fist, the hand merely needs to maintain this shape to remain on the hold. Part clenching the hand prior to placing it on the hold, results in the skin being pinched between the hand and the hold. If you are finding that you are getting blisters and calluses, place the hand onto the hold with your fingers outstretched. Then wrap your fingers around the hold. This will partially prevent this from occurring. Another tip to prevent this is to avoid slapping for the holds. With the combination of straight arms and good balance, you should not have to slap your hands onto the holds. Instead you should have time to gently place your hands which avoids the skin being pinched.

Slopers.

Most climbers hate slopers. They are rounded or "slopey" holds, and again, this is where the hold gets its name. They are formed where the rock is either very hard, like the Grit Stone in the Peak District. Over a long time, the hard Northern rock is weathered by the wind and the rain forming these rounded features. Likewise the softy Southern sandstone of Tunbridge Wells is very quickly eroded by the wind and rain, forming sloped round features. They feel very tenuous and because we feel like we cannot grip and pull with the hands, it can be very difficult to trust them. So how can we use them? Place your hand palm up to the ceiling with your fingers together. If you place your other thumb on your palm and gently squeeze, moving your thumb towards your fingers, you will notice that your skin starts to bunch or fold up at the base of the fingers. If you continue moving your thumb up the fingers, the skin will also create folds at each knuckle and at the fingertip. It is these folds, that provide us (limited) friction and hold us onto the sloper holds.

When using slopers, slap your whole hand on the best position on the hold (which will be looked at below) and hang down to create the folds of skin in the hands. The friction created by the folds of skin (with practise) will hold you onto the sloper hold. To spread your fingers, or to keep them together is personal preference. Personally I recommend that the fingers are kept together as much as possible as this not only creates friction on the joints, but also between the fingers, where they touch together. The best way to learn is to experiment and find what works best for you.

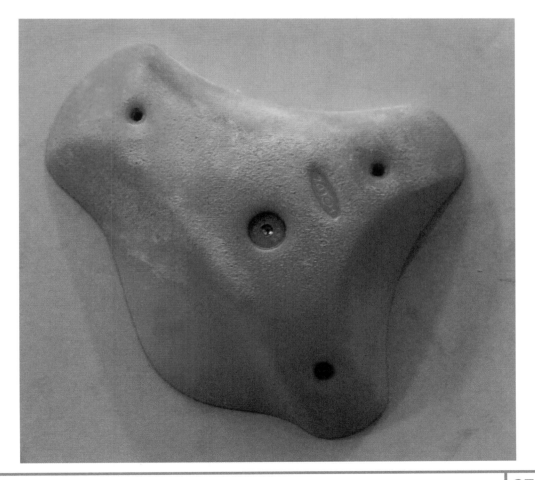

Small In-Cut Holds.

There are three ways in which we can use small in cut holds. Firstly, even if the hold looks un-useably small, avoid the temptation to place your fingernails up against the wall. Even in desperation it is a very poor contact. The part of the finger we want to place on the holds is the pad. Imagine that you are being fingerprinted by the hold. This is the best way to make contact between your fingers and the wall.

There are three ways in which we can use small holds in this way. Each way will feel more secure than the last enabling you to put more weight through the hand when you use it. While this is possible, injuries resulting from use of small holds are common even when the climber has good technique.

A note of caution. The more weight you are able to support with your fingers, the greater the chance of injury. When starting, or returning to climbing, be careful of "tweaks" or "ouchies". It is strongly recommended that you move onto smaller holds bit at a time. If you want to build up strength in the tendons and ligaments in the fingers, climb with smaller holds for the hands, but keep your feet on larger holds. You will slowly build up the tendon strength to use them safely. If you feel internal aching or sharper pains after climbing you may need to consider resting or taking professional advice to avoid injury. The sites of the pain are likely to be in the fingers, hand or forearm. Finger injures can be reasonably common when people improve and the size of the holds used reduces. Be careful, pay attention to what your body is telling you and seek advice as required. There are many advice pages and websites relating to climbing injuries for you to consider.

The Hang.

The first is to hang down under the hold, extending the fingers so you just hang off the pads. This is called a hang and is the easiest and safest way to use the hold. The issue with using the hold in this way is that when you pull down, a pivot point is created on the first knuckle and the finger tips are levered off the hold. The more you pull, the more the fingers are levered off the hold. This does not feel secure and in fact it feels like your fingers are being peeled off the holds.

The Half Crimp.

To make the hang feel more stable, we need to remove the pivot point in the fingers which will result in the fingers maintaining a positive contact. To achieve this, keep the pads on the hold the same way and raise up the middle knuckle in the fingers. You will notice that the pivot point has now been removed and rather than the fingers being levered off the front of the hold, they are now driven down and into the back of the hold. This feels much more secure and is called a **half crimp**.

The Full Crimp.

To make the half crimp feel even more secure, place your thumb over the knuckle of the first and or second finger (depending on how long your thumb is). The more the thumb pulls down onto the fingers, the more the fingers are driven onto the holds and the more secure the placement feels. This is called the **full crimp** and is the most secure way to hold onto smaller holds.

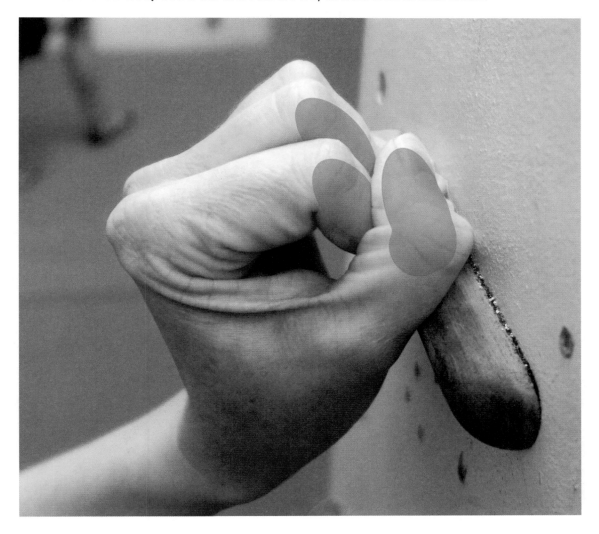

Pinches.

These holds are exactly as they sound. The fingers and thumb are on opposite sides of a hold and to use it, you need to squeeze to hold on. The further your centre of gravity is towards your fingers, the harder your thumb has to squeeze to hold on. The further to the finger side your centre of gravity gets, the harder and harder it is to hold. If you lean the other way, away from your fingers, the less the thumb has to grip to remain on the hold. It may be possible to lean all the way to the side, so the thumb can be completely removed. This creates a side pull as opposed to a pinch and because you do not have to squeeze at all to hold on, it is a much easier way of using this hold type.

Handhold Exercise.

Feel and hang each of the following holds. In this exercise it is best to start with holds which can be easily reached from the floor. Place your hand on slopers and feel the grip that can be gained by hanging down off the hand(s). Feel the difference in hold a pinch straight on and as a side pull - off to the side. Also feel the difference between the hang, half crimp and full crimp. Especially with smaller holds be careful and it is recommended that you do not take your feet off the floor unless you have other large supporting holds to reduce the weight on the crimping hand to reduce the risk of injury.

Orientation of the Holds and the Direction of Pull.

Not all holds have the best grip point orientated straight upwards. After all, if they all did; it would be like climbing a ladder and we would get bored quite quickly. The holds can be in any direction, even upside down. So we need to look at the holds and determine their orientation so we can hang off them effectively.

Consider the hold below. We can see that the best part of the hold which we wish to use is on top. Therefore the direction of pull is straight down. Trace a point straight down roughly 1 meter and form an imaginary dot on the wall. This should roughly translate to where your centre of gravity should be.

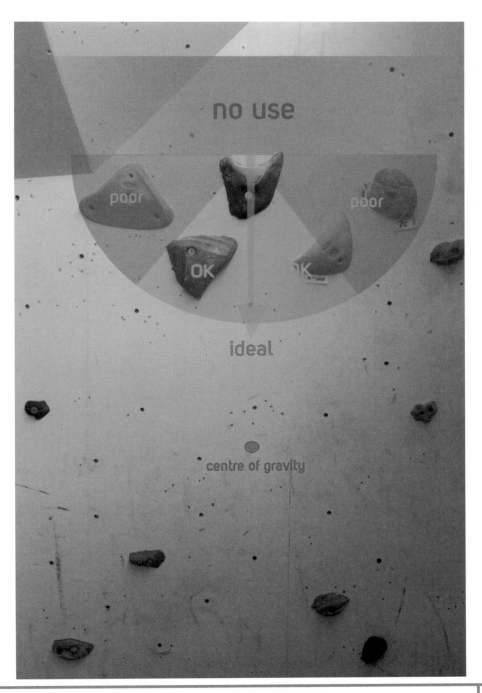

The direction of pull equally applies to holds which are pointing at differing angles. The diagram on the left shows a hold with the gripping area on the top right. Again make an arrow diagonally down and left which shows your centre of gravity should be below the hold and to the left hand side. Even if the holds are upside down, the same principle applies and can be used to work out the best way of using the hold. The photo on the right shows a hold which will need to be used from above. These are called underclings. Using this hold from below will turn it into a strenuous pinch and should be avoided.

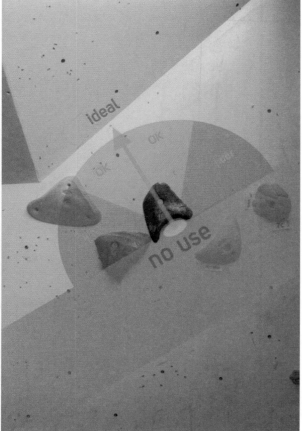

Working Out the Handholds.

Once the centre of gravity point has been established, it should be relatively easy to determine which hand can use the hold the most effectively. In both the examples above, the hold points the centre of gravity to the left, therefore the holds will be used with the right hand. If the direction of pull is to the right, the hold will be used with the left hand. There are times when the hold points straight down, and it could be used with either hand. In this scenario consider two things:

- Is the hold big enough to be used with both hands? If this is the case, the hold can be "matched". This allows either hand to move to the next hold in the sequence.
- If the hold is too small to match with both hands, consider the other holds around it to determine the sequence. This will ensure that the correct hand will use the hold and the rest of the climb can be completed without getting the hands out of sequence.

The picture below illustrates the principle of determining which hand should be place on to each hold.

Once this is undertaken, consider swinging straight arms from hold to hold and the path that your body will take similar to the exercises undertaken in the straight arms section.

Fine Tuning the Centre of Gravity.

It may have been noticed that in this photo, the centre of gravity does not quite match up with the direction of pull from the hold. To start off with, a rough guide to where the centre of gravity needs to be is fine. There are two reasons why we may need to refine where our centre of gravity needs to be.

Looking at the diagrams on the page below, we can see however that if we start to use the holds at differing angles, the hold gets less and less positive. On large "generous" holds, the best use can be quite a large angle. However if we lean the wrong way, positive holds can still feel poor. The further we lean away from the best angle to use the hold, the worse the hold becomes. Even a friendly jug can be turned in to a strenuous pinch. On smaller or less generous holds, the angle we need to use them can be drastically reduced and there can be times when there is only very specific areas to use the hold.

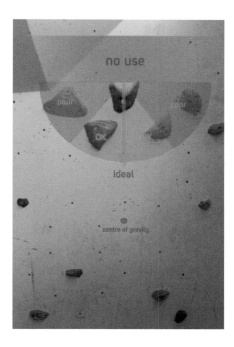

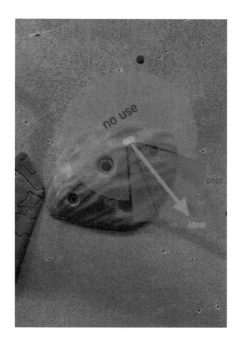

The second reason is to appreciate the most efficient way of moving between holds, we need to be able to determine more precisely where our centre of gravity will need to be.

When climbing with hips parallel to the wall and toes turned out to each side, the centre of gravity will be your bottom. To work out the exact centre of gravity when climbing in this style, Follow the direction of pull from the hold. The line should represent your arm. Follow this line and place a dot where your shoulder would be. From this first point, imagine another dot at the same height, roughly 30 cm straight towards your body. This point should be where your spine is between your shoulder blades. From your spine make a last dot one meter directly below it. This should be your bottom and will be your exact centre of gravity. When you climb with hips parallel to the wall, this skill will enable you to determine where your centre of gravity should be for any hold you use.

Once you have completed this with the starting hold, undertake it with the rest of the holds on the wall. Once this is completed, you should have determined your ideal centre of gravity point to hang each hold. All you now need to do is fill in the gaps that your centre of gravity will pass through from hold to hold. Similar to the more basic example in the previous section, consider your centre of gravity penduluming below each handhold as you swing from hold to hold across or up the route. This ensures that you climb with good balance and straight arms.

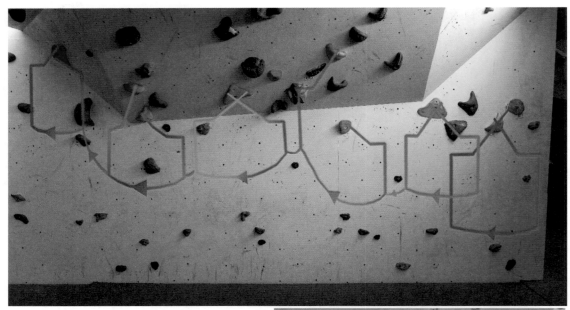

The diagram above demonstrates the exact place which your centre of gravity should pass when traversing or climbing across a route.

The same principle should be applied when the climb ascends the wall. Note again that if arms are kept straight and the centre of gravity is adjusted correctly, the climber will shift from side to side as they rise. This is preferable to a vertical ascent at the cost of climbing with bent arms.

Route Reading.

As we move across the wall or ascend the climb, the direction of pull principle remains the same. We can determine the best way to use each hold, which hand should be used and where our centre of gravity should be. We should look up the route considering each hold and move before leaving the floor. We are solving a physical puzzle - how do I easiest get from the start of the climb to the end? This is route reading. The ability to effectively read a route and plan our climb stops us from having to work it out as we go. Looking at beginner climbers, we can see them pause after each move to consider the next. This results in a jerky style of climbing with breaks in between moves. There is no flow or continual movement. As a result the climb takes longer and fatigue sets in. To resolve this, plan and execute. In effect read the route and have a go. If your plan was wrong, re-evaluate and have another go. This is just like musicians looking over a new piece of music before playing it, or looking over an IKEA instruction set before attempting to assemble the flat pack unit. Route reading gives you an overall plan, and a heads up for tricky sections.

Look at the top climbers in the world when in competitions or when climbing problems they have never seen before. They all plan from the floor before getting on and having a go. If they do, we should.

The problem is that there is limited coverage demonstrating climbers working out projects from the floor. The drama is all in the climbing. The plethora of videos available to us all want to stand out, demonstrating the exciting and awe inspiring climbing rather than the comparatively dull preparation, route reading or beta gathering undertaken in advance. An example is the video E11 with Dave McLeod. He did not need to route read Rhapsody to lead it cleanly when his successful ascent was undertaken. This was because the two previous years of preparation and climbing the route meant he knew the moves by heart. If you were to just watch the successful ascent, the route reading and working sections would be missed. The interesting and inspirational thing about the video is the continued reading, working and evaluation which occurred preceding the successful climb. Similarly, (but at a much lower level), when we have worked all the moves on a project for a lengthy period, it is likely we are able to know each move and the sequence of moves by memory. Working the same problem over and over gets us a step closer to completing that problem. Failing to route read climbs takes us a step away from improving this skill as we instil a gung ho, "lets see how we get on" attitude. This may be fun for some of us just wanting to jump on and have a play, but if you want to improve, this is one of the most important skills to master. Route reading, just like reading music or deciphering IKEA instructions is a skill that needs to be practised if we want correct execution first time.

When route reading, there are a number of things which we should look at and consider.

Read the climb three times. Each time we are looking at different aspects:

1. First run through, look for the hand holds. Determine the left and right hand holds to establish the basic sequence and where your centre of gravity needs to be.
2. Establish all the foot holds. Look around for holds which do not appear obvious. Take a step back if possible to view the whole climb especially if there are volumes / obstructions in the line of sight.
3. After you have tied on or sat at the sit start - run quickly through the whole climb again so that it is fresh in your mind.

Ongoing exercise: Plan EVERY CLIMB BEFORE CLIMBING IT! it is as simple as that.

1. Route Read
2. Climb
3. Evaluate

Was your plan correct? Did you have to make minor or major changes? Were there things you missed? Keep planning, especially on routes you can climb easily as the more you use this skill, the better and more experienced you will become. Route reading is a slow, ongoing process and the benefits are that when you climb a route, you will keep the "surprises" to a minimum. You will gain confidence on routes and start to identify the hard moves and crux sequences on a climb. More on this will be covered in section 3.

Chapter 4 - Set 2: Introducing Twisting.

Introduction to Efficient Twisting.

The exercises and skills in Set 1 develop the skills required to effectively climb the vast majority of climbs on a slab. They are equally transferrable to vertical walls. However when the wall starts to tilt backwards into an overhang, they are less and less effective. On a slab, we keep our hips parallel to the wall and standing up on the higher foot results in us pushing straight up the wall. By contrast, if our hips remain parallel to the wall on an overhang, when we push with our legs our centre of gravity is pushed out, away from the wall. To make the next move, we have to pull ourselves back into the wall with our arms. The steeper the overhang the more drastic the effect.

To change this, we need to do something different in order to gain height. We need to learn to twist.

In the photos on the page below, we can see the climber on the top row climbing as we normally would do on a slab. Both feet are pointed out to the side, using the inside edge, and the legs are ready to push. The middle photo demonstrates when pushing with the legs, his centre of gravity is pushed away from the wall and the weight is transferred onto his arms. In the third photo, we can see the amount he has to pull with his arms to reach for the next hold. This looks clearly inefficient and despite being strong, the climber described this position as "just horrible".

In the lower row of photos, the climber sets up in the same position, however in the middle photo he twists his hips into the wall. This keeps his centre of gravity close to the wall for more effective pushing with the legs. In the last photo, he twists his shoulders into the wall to reach for the next hold rather than pulling with the arms, making the move much easier.

Outside Edge.

The most useful and the "go to" technique when looking to transition onto steeper walls is the outside edge. Getting it to work well for you is difficult to master and requires a great deal of practise. Start on traverse walls, then move on to easy vertical walls and expect to take many weeks of practise. Expect that because this style of climbing requires constant leaning back on the arms, it is likely to feel alien and may feel like **more** weight is being put onto the arms. However in the long run it is physically much easier than pulling yourself into the wall with each move, and using bent arms.

Exercise: Finding the Ideal Rest Position.

Use large holds within easy reach of the floor.

- Use opposite hand and foot.
- Hang down off a handhold with a straight arm.
- Twist the shoulders almost 90° to the wall facing towards the hand which is holding on.
- The remaining hand can be anywhere comfortable not on a hold.
- Place the outside edge of the opposite foot on a hold **directly below** the hand hold.
- Use the 5 stage foot placement; the same as in Set 1, however use the middle 3 toes to gain a good outside edge placement.
- Ensure the remainder of the foot is slightly angled, maybe 45° to the wall.
- Hips should now be roughly 90 degrees to the wall in line with the shoulders.
- Lean back and down, hanging off the straight arm sinking down into the rest position.
- Point your other leg out away from you. This is likely to be around the same height as the foot hold. This leg will counterbalance you and make the position stable so there is no swing.

Repeat with the opposite hand and foot. This is the least strenuous way to hold on and can be considered the default or rest position.

Coaching:

When watching a climber in this position, ensure that there are only two points of contact **using the holds**. eg Left hand and Right foot. The climber should be sinking down into a low rest position. The leg on the hold should have minimal pressure and should not be attempting to stand up. The pressure should be similar to squatting down, and the climber should look like they are squatting side onto the wall. Arms must be straight as to bend and pull in this position will put a great deal of weight on the bicep.

It is favourable to attempt the dominant hand first, which will be easier to gain the correct position and provide reassurance that this can be achieved with the weaker arm. When swapping over, find differing holds which allow the hang to be easily trialled on the other hand and foot.

Exercise: Feeling the Variations.

Two factors drastically affect the amount of weight felt on the arm when twisting into the wall. The combination of the two following exercises will illustrate the optimal position of the foot for an outside edge.

The lateral location of the foothold -

- Further away from the climber, the balance point is lowered. This means more weight comes onto the arm, however the position is more stable. The counterbalancing foot is raised to compensate.

- Closer to the climber, there is less weight on the arm, however there is much more chance of swinging out or barn-dooring. The counterbalancing foot needs to clamp hard on to the wall to stop the swing. The counterbalancing foot is lowered to compensate.

Using a similar or the same large handhold as the initial practise exercise, start in the balanced outside edge rest position. Step off the wall, and using the same hand hold, select a foothold slightly (15 cm) further away from the initial foothold. This should be ata similar height to the original. Hang this position. Notice that more weight is transferred to the arm and the counterbalancing foot needs to be placed higher on to the wall to balance effectively. Once this position has been felt, repeat with the foot further and further away. Each position will feel more and more strenuous.

Returning to the natural rest position. Repeat the exercise, however this time moving the foot closer and closer to your body. This should feel slightly easier on the arm, however it will become more and more difficult to keep from swinging around to the side. This is because your balance is become less stable and the counterbalancing foot (and core in the extreme end of the exercise) will have to work very hard to prevent the swing round.

The **height of the foothold** will drastically affect the amount of weight on the hand / arm.

- The higher the foothold, the more "push" that can be achieved, but more weight is placed onto the arm.
- The lower the foothold, the less weight is on the arm, but less push is available from the leg.

The ideal height of the foothold can easily be tested on an arête, corner of the wall or even a doorframe you are able to lean off. Place your hand onto the arête reasonably high, probably just above head height. Place the outside edge of your opposite foot at the base of the arête and lean back to hang the rest position. In this high position, there should be very little weight on the hand, but because the leg is already reasonably straight there is little height able to be gained in this position.

Slide your hand slowly down the wall, testing differing positions. This should be undertaken in roughly 15 - 30 cm increments. You should continue as low as you can, leaning back on each position until there is around a 30-45 cm gap between the hand and foot. Note the happy medium, probably around chest height, where there is moderate weight on the arm, however there is still a significant amount of push enabled with the bent leg.

Coaching:

It is important for the climber to undertake these tests prior to attempting to climb, as this will easily illustrate the differences between each position. The climber will then be able to appreciate that appropriate foothold selection can make a drastic impact on whether the move feels achievable or not. In the long run, this appreciation of the variations speeds up the learning of the outside edge technique. Ensure that each variant is held for at least 5 seconds as this will give enough time to process and remember the differences.

Exercise: Moving from Hold to Hold.

Now that the rest position has been learned, we need to learn to move between the holds as efficiently as possible. Having hung the rest position with both hands, we need to move between these rest positions so that throughout the climb we move from rest, to rest, to rest position. Consider the basics of straight arms in set 1. This involved hanging down and swinging from hold to hold with your centre of gravity penduluming under straight arms. Practise an easy traverse to remind yourself of this principle. Once this has been completed, undertake the same traverse using only the outside edge of your foot.

1. Hang the rest position. (Assuming a left hand outside edge position climbing right to left).
2. Place your right hand on to the next hold. (Still facing to the left).
3. Move your left foot onto the next ideal foot hold - directly below the right hand. (This may be a foot swap).
4. Allow gravity to pull you round - go with it and end facing to the right. (Sometimes a nudge round is needed).
5. Remove the right foot, and find the counterbalance point.
6. Remove left hand and hang down for 5 seconds to reset and recall the rest position.

Now you are holding with the right hand in the opposite rest position.

1. Place your left hand on the next hold.
2. Push your bottom away from the wall with the left foot creating space for step 3.
3. Step your right foot through onto the next foot hold. (Directly below the left hand).
4. Twist and face to the left. (While twisting around, the left foot will come off the hold).
5. Stretch out the left foot to find the counterbalance point.
6. Remove the right hand.
7. You are back to the original rest position. Repeat & repeat until the end.

Video 10 demonstrates how people learning this technique can be easily coached into the correct position and in the second clip, how it should look when practised.

The outside edge technique takes a great deal of practise to feel natural. Rather than climbing straight to the goal i.e. the next handhold, we are swinging off straight arms and almost taking a round about way of getting there. Just think, is a less strenuous detour more or less efficient than an energetic direct route?

It can be learned effectively by demanding a handshake or a high 5 after getting into each rest position. Adults may prefer to shake out the forearm or chalk up. Teenagers may send a tweet. Whatever technique is employed, ensure that a hand is removed and rest is taken and recognised as an easy position to hang.

Once you have correctly used the outside edge to traverse in both directions, a vertical climb can be attempted. You should be comfortable leaning back off the hand holds, always using the outside edge and twisting to the correct side before progressing. The two main problems to tackle when we start climbing up are demonstrated in Video 11.

- Standing up too soon. Wait until you are into the correct rest position with the hand which will be removed from the previous hold. Only then are you in the correct rest position. If you attempt to stand up prior to removing the hand, it is likely that you will not be twisting to the full extent that you need to. This will result in pulling rather than leaning back on a straight arm. It is also easier to get out of sync if you do not stop in the rest position each time.
- Standing up too far. When learning to twist, people almost always push further than they need to reach to get to the next hold. If you push too far, when the hand is placed onto the hold, you will have a bent arm which will encourage you to pull. Or you push too high, then sink back down on to a straight arm. This looks jerky and is not a smooth ascent of the wall.

To prevent both these problems, when in the resting position, before you think about pushing up, raise the moving hand up to the next hold. Undertaking this will prevent both the problems above:

- You will only be able to slowly reach up when you are in the rest position. Therefore it is much easier to maintain straight arms.
- When you raise your hand towards the next hold, you can see how far you need to push. This will stop you standing too high on the holds and getting above where you need to be to effectively use a straight arm.

Coaching:

Ensure that the climber gets to the rest position each time. They should be able to stop and rest on a straight arm at the end of each move. When coaching this, it can be ensured by telling the climber to chalk up, wave, high 5 or pretend to clip at the end of every move. Having the climber appreciate this position is key to them comprehending twisting.

Classic problems with twisting are getting the hands and feet out of sync. If the climber faces away from their arm, they will be hanging on a bent arm which is extremely energy intensive. If something does get out of sync, it is best that the climber stops. Returns to the correct rest position, then attempts the move again. It is important that errors are corrected **as they occur** so that the technique is learned properly. A common cause of this is when hands match or swap on a hold, people tend not to twist on one of the moves. To resolve this, as above: stop, reset and continue.

Other issues include only twisting one way. People generally have a dominant hand and are more likely to comfortably twist using that hand. They are less likely to adopt the twisting position with the other, weaker hand. An easy way to counteract this is to ensure that the climber rests after each move in the correct rest position. If they are not in this position, it will be very hard to hold the position for 3-5 seconds especially with only one hand on the wall. Breaking the climb down into individual moves separated by rests helps cement each move. Climbers may always practise hanging off their weaker hand whilst close to the floor or on a low, easy traverse to increase their confidence and ability to undertake this position.

Sometimes climbers cannot visualise stepping and twisting their body across their stride, which is the position we need to get into. It is not how we walk (continually facing forwards) and may cause confusion. Sometimes the analogy of fashion models walking on a catwalk, crossing their feet and turning side to side with each stride can be sufficient to make people comprehend this aspect.

Lastly, because people generally do not climb leaning back on their arms, this is likely to be tiring. Even on easy routes on a vertical wall, they are likely to get tired after just a few climbs. It is better to undertake 3 to 5 perfect moves, twisting the correct way and learning what works, than it is to undertake some good moves interspaced with mistakes. The more moves that are made correctly with no mistakes, the quicker the technique is learned. Therefore the climbers goal should be to focus on making the moves correctly rather than reaching the top of the climb. By climbing in this way, the climber will build up the differing muscle strength within a month or so with continued practise.

Flagging.

To undertake a flag the upper body remains the same as the above. The shoulders are still twisted 90 degrees to the wall and the climber should be looking along a straight arm to the hand which is holding on.

The difference is it is the same hand and foot that are used. This results in the foot which is on the hold being on an inside edge rather than an outside edge as above. The counterbalancing foot, just like when undertaking an outside edge needs to find balance by being straightened out past the handhold.

When flagging the foot out, this can be done above or below the foot on the wall:

- Below the foothold, as photo 1, there is less push that can be undertaken before the counterbalancing leg stops the other from properly straightening. Having the counterbalancing leg below however feels safer due to being able to be easily removed in the event of a fall.
- Above the foothold, as photo 2, more push can be gained, however it feels more scary and like it will be trapped in the event of a fall, preventing the climber from jumping down effectively (especially when bouldering).

The principles regarding height and lateral location of the foothold are identical to that of outside edge mentioned above. Complete the same exercises as the outside edge, however this time use an inside edge flag.

You are ready to progress to the next set when you have a good understanding of changing your centre of gravity and are comfortable leaning back on your arms. You should be able to complete a traverse and an easy vertical climb (4-5) using effective twisting, always facing the correct way, keeping arms straight and pushing with your legs.

Chapter 5 - Set 3: Refinement.

Set 3 introduces the final efficiencies and fine tuning of the techniques learned in Sets 1 and 2. Some of the techniques will not take too long to master, others will evolve and develop over the rest of your climbing career. This is because once the principles have been learned, you have all the tools you need to climb walls of all angles as efficiently as possible, from slabs to vertical walls and overhangs. You need to select the most efficient tool to tackle the next move of the route. There may be subtle differences and approaches and it is only experience and knowing what works best for you that will determine which technique you should utilise on any given move. This is why the next section will take the rest of your climbing career to master as your body, strength and experience evolves and changes over time. This section can be broken down in to techniques and skills.

Techniques:

- Pivoting, rather than moving your feet.
- Drop knees.
- Exaggerated twisting.
- Dynamic moves (Dynos.)
- Bouldering sit starts.
- Heel and Toe Hooks.

Skills:

- Advanced Route Reading.
- Appropriate twisting on a route.
- Finding and use of rests.
- Appropriate clipping position (if leading.)
- Appropriate use of speed on a climb.
- Controlling fear - Especially whilst on lead.

Techniques:

Pivoting - (Rather Than Moving Feet).

Once we have learned to use the outside edge and the flag appropriately, it may be possible to undertake two or three smaller moves, without removing our foot from the foot hold. If we think about climbing a route with smaller moves, keeping your feet on the holds may be easier than moving them with each small move that is made. This will involve keeping a pivoting foot on a hold and twisting the foot along with the body when we face the correct way.

When we learn to place our feet on the holds, we practise one touch, perfect placements and concentrate on the foot remaining on the hold in the same position to ensure its placement remains good. The principle of pivoting considers whether it is more efficient to undertake a foot swap, or a pivot – twisting the direction of the foot on the hold.

In the photo above, there are multiple handholds within easy reach of a single foothold. It is important to note that the holds are reasonably vertical above the foothold. Consider the lateral placement of the foot in relation to the handhold. The further out to each side the next hand hold will be, the more strenuous using a pivot will be. In some circumstances moving the foot to a better placed hold will be more efficient. In general however, swapping feet will put weight on the arms and consider this pivoting alternative, especially if the next hold is not a long way out to the side.

Pivoting and rotating one foot rather than swapping feet, enables us to maintain the correct twisting position while reducing the load being taken onto our arms each time. The aim is that the foot remains on the foot hold, however pivots from an outside edge to an inside edge flag and vice versa. This pivot is undertaken as the body twists from side to side according to the handholds, considered in Set 2. Video 12 illustrates how ineffective constant foot swapping can be and compares the pivoting principle. In the second part of the video the problem is re-climbed, demonstrating how effective the pivoting principle is at reducing weight from the arms. Notice the foot pivots change between an outside edge and a flag without being removed from the hold. This maintains the body position on the wall and reduces weight from the arms with the removal of the foot swap.

Pivot Exercise 1- Pivoting on One Foot.

Pick an easy route and practise. Start on large holds where precision with the foot is not imperative. You want to look for a climb which ascends straight up, pretty much a ladder. This will make the balance easier. You should find that while you may be required to pull with the hands a little while pivoting, compare whether this is easier than swapping feet or using a higher foot hold. The size of the holds can be reduced in size later and utilising a pivoting technique, maintaining precision on small holds requires continued practise. When the foot pivots, especially on small holds it can be easy for the foot to slip off. To counteract this, when placing the foot on the hold, ensure there is sufficient room on the side you need to pivot on to.

Coaching:

A sufficiently easy route should be climbed. The route should be on a vertical / slightly overhanging wall. Climbs with (numerous) hand matches and many small moves are ideal for this technique as the climber will still need to twist without changing the foot holds. This type of route should:

- Allow for straight arms.
- Encourage the pivot.
- Keep enough weight on the foot so there is less chance of it slipping off the hold.

The climber will need to keep counterbalancing with the other leg. The counterbalancing leg will point side to side with the direction of the twist. It is almost like a can can on the wall.

Pivot Exercise 2 - Using Both Feet.

Once you have gained the pivoting principle using one foot, consider whether two feet are better than one. When using outside edge and flagging, you have been climbing primarily using one foot on a hold and the other counterbalancing rather than being placed on a hold. The simple reason for this is that the techniques are absorbed quicker when only one foot is used. These outside edge and flagging techniques have now been learned, so rather than placing the outstretched foot against the wall, where the route allows, place it onto a hold. You will have both feet facing the same way, your closest foot will use an outside edge and the foot which is further away will use an inside edge. Now we are back to the age old rule of three points of contact on the wall. When we twist from side to side, we can pivot both feet to maintain the correct twist and straight arms. If you are familiar with skiing, pivoting both feet can be likened to parallel turns, twisting your feet across your body. If you are more familiar with golf or hockey, it can be likened to before and after photos of taking a swing. When you set up, both feet face forwards. After the pivot, both feet point across the body towards the hand which is holding you onto the wall. There are also times where the foot holds are either side of the hand hold. To use only one foot would prove strenuous because the foot hold is not directly beneath the hand hold. In this circumstance, the use of two feet, pivoting both of them as the body twists is a much easier way of climbing.

Video 13 demonstrates the advantages of pivoting with both feet rather than solely using one foot.

The important thing is to practise this technique and gain confidence and experience in what works best for you. You should find that when this technique is learned and executed effectively, the least amount of weight is placed on to your arms. This can especially be felt on overhanging walls, however it is also very effective on vertical climbs.

This style of pivoting is more advanced than just using one leg and one arm as practised in Set 2, and it is much easier to get out of sync with this method and revert to pulling. If this happens, reset and concentrate on continually facing the correct way.

Coaching:

This technique can be most effectively taught and practised on the traverse wall. The climber should set up as if they were practicing a balanced traverse detailed in section 1. Ensure they have both feet as wide, or wider than their hands. This time however, the climber should twist from side to side ensuring they are in the twisted rest position rather than keeping their hips parallel to the wall as in the initial exercise. If they are twisting and moving their feet effectively, they should face side to side as if they were only using one foot and either swapping feet or stepping through. This technique will take a great deal of practise to cement. It will be likely to feel alien after getting used to twisting only using one foot, however it should feel much less energy intensive given time.

Drop Knees.

Drop knees are a simple extension of pivoting on the footholds. Notice that when we pivot, to maintain a straight arm the body is twisted side on to the wall and both knees will bend, pointing the same way. This looks similar to Egyptian depictions, and is where the drop knee gets its other name - the Egyptian. Exaggeration of the outside edge, combined with a high foot hold forces the knee lower and lower until the knee is below the foot. Once the knee is below the foot, this is a drop knee.

To practise this technique, find a slightly overhanging wall. Get into a balanced position with both hands in between your feet. Determine which hand will move to the next hold. Place the foot on the same side as the moving hand onto a slightly higher and / or wider foot hold. Place the foot with an inside edge, then with a similar action as pivoting both feet, as you twist your shoulders and hips, roll your foot to the outside edge and drop your knee down to the floor. This will result in the hips being twisted completely into the wall and your hand easily being able to move to the next hold. The difference between the drop knee and pivoting is that when you place the foot onto the hold, with the drop knee, you will need to be more careful that the foot does not rotate off the hold. This is because you are pivoting the foot much further than before. You may therefore wish to place your foot on the closest edge of the hold to you, allowing maximum space to roll the foot onto the outside edge. This may indeed be the side of the hold rather than the top. Placing the foot onto the side of the hold may feel strange, but because you are pushing outwards onto the hold rather than down it may be a better placement. Compare this to bridging in the next section. Because there is more of an outwards push it is almost like creating a bridge, albeit maybe a poor one.

Exercise: Starting to Exaggerate the Pivot.

On a route, form a triangle between a hand and both feet. Using the opposite foot to the hand, step onto a slightly higher hold with an inside edge. Pivot the foot while bending the knee in and down. You should notice that you are twisted into the wall, facing your holding hand. Your higher foot will be behind you and in some cases, you are almost sitting on it. Once your knee points down to the floor below the foot, it is a drop knee. Many people feel like that they have undertaken a great drop knee, however unless the knee is below the foot, this is more like an exaggerated pivot. Once the knee is below the foot you will feel the benefit as the hips are forced into the twisted position. The second clip of <u>video 12</u>contains pivots in the first section and a drop knee higher up the climb.

So why should we create such a weird move or position to be in? The basic answer is that when the drop knee is properly executed, pressure is created between the feet and the hips are forced into the wall. This removes weight from the hands, and when the holds are small, especially when on a steep overhang, it is likely to make the difference between making the next move and falling off. This requires a moderate amount of flexibility in the knee and hip joints, therefore starting small and slowly exaggerating the move is strongly suggested. Again, it is likely that we will have a stronger side, so practise with both and train any weaknesses.

Coaching:

Drop knee positions can be hard to spot from the floor. Looking for triangles of holds on the wall will make this easier. The next hand hold will be likely to be above (or wider than) the higher foot. Undertaking the pivoting technique first will ease the climber into undertaking lower and lower knee positions which will eventually turn into a drop knee. Trying to manufacture the position can be difficult, and if the holds are too small or the position too difficult, they are unlikely to feel the benefit. Again concentrate on the climber correctly learning the pivoting concept underpinning the move rather than forcing a drop knee in a strenuous position where the benefit is likely to be lost.

Exaggerated Twisting.

One significant benefit of using the outside edge and leaning back on straight arms is the ability to place the feet much higher than when you are in a vertical position with hips square to the wall. To briefly test this, use two holds around chest height and see how far up you are able to place your foot on a hold beneath your hands. To compare this, lean out to one side. Try placing your foot onto the holds and see how much further up the wall you are able to place the foot.

Especially when using side pulls and underclings, a higher foot allows a much greater upwards push. We can then make much larger moves than is possible if our hips are parallel to the wall. Of course making larger moves is more strenuous, however because we miss out a move or two, it can be more efficient than making a larger number of smaller moves. On harder routes with longer stretches, this may be the only way to reach the next hold.

When making larger moves, twist completely into the wall. The use of core strength will keep you stable as you twist in and push up with the feet. The arm which will go onto the next hold should roll completely across your body to ensure that the twist is exaggerated as much as possible. Imagine that you are rolling over and giving yourself a cuddle. When the upwards push is completed, this arm "wind mills" round, brushing past your ear to be placed onto the next hold. As soon as your hand is on the hold, reposition your feet and hang the rest position.

Especially on very steep walls, this exaggerated technique will enable you to climb maintaining a smooth technical pushing style which saves a great deal of muscle strength. It may be noted that the greater the height that is gained, the more the arm which is holding on seems to bend. As we roll over the arm, it will lock across our chest or stomach and bend at the elbow. Initially, when learning outside edge technique we learn not to bend our arms, however this is to avoid the arm bending with the elbow pointing away from us in the "hands up" position. When we twist in this way, because our arm bends across our chest or stomach, our weight is still taken by the skeleton rather than the musculature and we are effectively still on a straight arm. This is because the arm is locked in this position by the body and forms an arm lock where little strength is required to remain holding on.

Practise larger moves, still made in a static, controlled fashion. You should be able to pause at almost any part of the move, and reverse the move if it proves a stretch too far. Once you have practised on a vertical wall, try it out on an overhang. Remember the shoulders rolling over are even more important on overhangs as the twist locks the arm in place so little strength is used.

This principle is the same if the next hand hold is off to one side. Again the temptation is to pull in, then reach out to grab to the next hold. If we twist and just lean back, it is likely that the hold will be just behind us. Just like the above, roll the shoulders to lock the arm in place, then wind mill or back stroke the arm behind us to reach the hold. This should feel so much easier than pulling.

Video 14 demonstrates a boulder problem with some larger reaches made in control.

Coaching:

When making larger moves, climbers tend to feel like they need to pull and slap for the next hold. In reality, if they are twisting, leaning off a straight arm, all that needs to happen is the legs need to push up and the hold is reachable whilst remaining in control.

When coaching larger exaggerated twisting, the climber should firstly be instilled with the concept that straight arms will provide greater reach than bent arms. Simply put, bent arms on larger moves actually pull us further away from the target hold making the move seem impossibly far. Twisting and leaning back on straight arms will provide a far greater reach and effective coaching of this is likely to resolve many problems relating to height and reach issues.

Bridging, Palming and Planting.

When there is a reachable gap between walls, we can use both walls to climb up. Chimneys and corners are perfect examples, however even a slight protrusion from the rock or smearing on both walls can be used. Bridges can make for great rest stops, especially if the holds are positive, however there are equally many bridging routes which are marginal at best. Starting with the basics of spanning gaps, there are various ways in which this can be undertaken.

A bridge is created when your body spans a gap; just like a bridge. When climbing a chimney there may be different parts of our body in contact with the walls: feet, bottom, back, shoulder or even head. These are all bridges. Depending on the route, either the inside or outside edges of the feet can be used depending on the style of and relative angles of the walls climbed. When your legs span a gap and a rest is undertaken, as much as is possible weight should be equalised between the feet. This is assuming that the holds are equally positive. The less positive each hold is, the more weight will need to be transferred to that foot to ensure that it does not slip. When moving each foot up the wall, pressure needs to be applied to the other foot. This releases weight from the moving foot so it can be placed onto the next hold or smeared higher up the wall. When this is undertaken, both feet can be loaded again so another bridging rest can be undertaken. This is a similar principle to how the slab is climbed; the further your weight is transferred over each foot, the less is placed onto the hands.

When both feet are on one wall and your back is on another, to gain height, the heel of one foot is likely to be placed under your bottom. This provides sufficient grip to push. Once your back is replaced higher on the wall, this forms enough grip to walk the feet higher up the opposing wall. This process can be repeated as necessary.

Palming is where the palm of the hand is used to create pressure on the wall rather than using the holds. It is a similar principle to smearing, but with your hands: the angle the hand pushes onto the wall, combined with the amount of weight placed onto the hand determines the stability of the placement. Low or wide placements with minimal pressure are likely to slip. More central placements with your weight pushing into the wall are less likely to slip. Like smearing, where possible attempt to keep the arms straight and locked. This will avoid using the arm muscles which will get tired very quickly if pushing off the legs. Palming could also be used instead of the heel of the foot when using a back bridge detailed above. Again, they are not used to push up the route, more to stabilise the push from the legs until the weight is transferred to the back and feet.

Planting is where the hand is much lower and gets "planted" low onto a hold or the wall. This can be utilised when the foot is coming up to match the same hold as the hand or in place of a foot hold which is too high or inaccessible to use. The arm is locked straight, with the body weight pushing into the hold to gain grip. In this position, either the higher hand is able to reach another hold, or the foot is able to match the same hold as the hand, releasing it to move up.

Starting Boulder Problems.

The common problem we hear with bouldering starts is that a lack of strength is responsible for the inability to hang the start holds or make the first move. It is expected that because boulder routes are generally more powerful, the start is no exception. However, look at experienced climbers. Is there something we are missing? There is an age old myth that if the starting holds can be reached while sitting on the floor, the climber must start the problem using a sit start. Even until recently I carried this myth through my climbing career and in some places found that the sit start on many boulder problems could be drastically harder than the rest of the climb, and in others it could be undoable. In many circumstances not undertaking a sit start would have been more efficient but blinded by this unwritten rule, I had been making it hard for myself for years.

So what is acceptable when starting boulder problems? The International Federation of Sport Climbing prescribes:

"Each boulder shall have a clearly marked start which shall consist of:

a) Marked handhold(s) for hands; and

b) Marked foothold(s) for feet"

While these rules and centres marking or tagging the starting holds may tell us what holds are acceptable to use, it still does not answer the question: If the holds can be reached while sitting on the floor, does a sit start have to be undertaken?

It is generally accepted across the climbing and route setting community that each problem should be climbed in the easiest possible way. The use of features, arêtes and volumes for example are generally allowed unless prescribed otherwise. This equally applies to the start of the problem. As long as the climbers hands and feet are in contact with the starting holds and this position can be maintained to make the starting move, a sit, squat, stand or in some cases a jump may be the only way to start the boulder problem.

To help you decide how to commence a boulder problem there are a number of factors to consider:

1. How high up are the starting holds. Can they even be reached from a sitting position?
2. Determine the direction of pull of the hand holds and where your centre of gravity will need to be placed to use them the most effectively.
3. How low are the holds? (The more crunched up you are, the harder a crouched position is likely to be to maintain).
4. Is it possible to push down off the starting holds? This may be favourable to getting underneath and sit starting the problem.

Video 15 contains clips where either a sit start or a squat could successfully be used. For the first two problems, they are successfully climbed using either a sit start or a squat. In the last problem, the climbers employ differing ways of starting it. The first is able to undertake a sit start, finding that laying back off the arms is preferable to a very powerful compression. The second climber finds that a squat is much more preferable to the sit start. Your preferential style of climbing will determine how you approach a boulder start where either could be used.

Sit Starts:

Accomplishing sit starts successfully utilises the skills of direction of pull, and a combination of outside edge, flagging, pivoting or drop knees to execute the move to avoid using brute strength.

Determine the starting handholds and plot the direction of pull, then plant your centre of gravity (sit down) in the best possible position.

From this seated stance, place the hands and feet onto the appropriate holds. From here, rather than pulling in with the arms or pushing with the legs, merely raise your pelvis and you will lift off the floor. Now you are on the problem. In this circumstance, it is more successful to pull onto an outside edge, however equally it could be an inside edge flag that works most effectively.

If there are two foot holds or a foothold and smear on an adjoining volume / wall, both feet can be used. In this position, the closest foot is likely to be an outside edge. Again, raise the hips to avoid pulling and get into either a position of sitting on a foot or between the feet in a drop knee. Now, in this rest position, you can climb the rest of the problem.

Video 16 demonstrates a range of sit starts utilising variations of this technique.

Squat Starts:

Holds which cannot be reached while sitting on the floor will have to be started from a squat. There are also times when a sit start may be a very inefficient way of starting the route. The holds could be farther apart or using the starting holds as a plant, by pushing down onto them, may be significantly easier than making a strenuous first move, smearing or having to swap feet after the sit start is completed. Underclings, where you need to be above the holds to use it effectively are more likely to be started successfully as a squat start. Determine the direction of pull to use the holds the most effectively, then squat to place your centre of gravity at that point. Lastly, put your hands and feet on the starting holds and you are now on the problem in the easiest way. Video 17 shows where squat or standing starts would be more beneficial to undertake rather than sit starts.

Conversely, if the handholds are poor and the centre of gravity needs to be lowered to hang the starting holds, a sit start may be the only way to make the first move. This is illustrated in video 18. Because the holds are poor slopers, to undertake the start move the climber's centre of gravity needs to be placed below and to the left of the starting handhold. This is easily undertaken in the first video. In the second clip, the climber changes to a squat, however because the holds are so poor, he has to change the footholds to be below the handhold and cannot get his centre of gravity into the correct position. This makes the handholds so poor that they are unable to be used and as a result he falls off the start.

It is only experience and practise that will tell you which is the easiest way of undertaking any boulder problem. If you are aspiring to flash problems and especially if you wish to undertake competitions, correctly identifying what is the best way of starting a boulder problem is imperative.

Coaching:

Most bouldering starts are not effective because the climber fails to position themselves correctly on the starting holds. Establishing the exact position the centre of gravity should be is the key to success. If climbers are slightly off, especially on small or poor holds, the increase in strength required is tremendous. To coach effective boulder starting moves specifically, the climber needs refinement on the direction of pull on small holds and fine tuning their twisting skills. If their route reading, twisting or outside edge footwork requires improvement, it will make the sit start much more physical than it needs to be.

Heel / Toe Hooks and the Heel Rock Over.

Heel and toe hooks are most commonly used when climbing arêtes, steep walls or when passing a lip on roofed sections.

To start using heel hooks, climb a route with an arête and holds around the side of the wall. When leaning away from the arête, place the closest foot around the corner. The heel of the foot should be placed onto the near side of the hold. When undertaking this, the toe should be pointed up (like a child breaking ice in a puddle but more controlled). Once the heel is placed onto the hold (photo 1), the toe rotates down (photo 2). This is the reason for the heel being required to be placed on the near side of the hold. Rotating the toe down has a number of benefits, the heel is rolled into a more beneficial angle to hook on the hold, the calf muscle is engaged allowing more pull, and on some moves, the inside edge of the shoe comes in to contact with the wall. The inside edge cams the foot into the wall creating maximum contact between foot and wall and increasing the stability and grip of the placement.

Once these have been practised on an easy angled arête, attempt similar placements on a more vertical or overhanging wall.

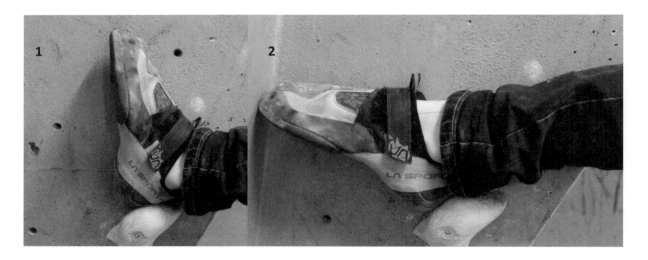

When passing roofs or lips, they can be used in much the similar way. The sole disadvantage with using these types of placements is that the hips are forced parallel to the wall / floor and much of the weight is focussed again onto your arms. There are times that twisting or drop knees may be more effective, however you will need to determine what will work best for you and your strengths.

Toe hooks can be introduced in a similar format. On an arête, preferably an easy angled one, attempt to lean away from the edge and place the top of the foot around the corner, onto the hold. This time, point the toes prior to the placement and then pull your foot up (back towards your knee) when placed on the hold. This provides the greatest friction available as the toes / top of your foot is pulling back onto the hold or wall. Photo 1 shows the pointing prior to being placed onto the wall. Photo 2 shows the toes pulling back for the optimum contact.

The main difference between the heel and the toe hook, is either foot can be used to undertake a toe hook around the edge of an arête / roof lip. If it is the foot further away from the arête, it is likely to hook lower allowing a lesser lean. With the foot on the same side of the arête, it can be hooked higher, allowing the body to lean further off the hold which may be required to reach holds further away while still remaining balanced.

Similar to the exercises for heel hooks, practise on more and more overhanging walls to gain full mastery of this technique.

The heel hook rock over is a technique that can be used best on vertical and overhanging walls. It is most likely to be used on reasonably large holds to make a move easier or take a rest. In places where you may need to undertake a rock over with your toe, instead, try placing the heel of the shoe onto the hold and rocking over the heel instead. The same as a toe rock over on the slab, the centre of gravity should be put directly over the heel to maintain balance. What you may notice with the use of the heel rather than the toe is that because of the way that the front of the foot cams into the wall (as discussed in heel hooks), this can take a dramatic amount of weight off the arms. In some cases, it may be possible to remove both hands and take a full rest. This will require a fair amount of practise! In the pictures below, the climber in the first picture positions his heel onto the top corner of the hold. Note that rather than placing the foot on the far corner of the hold, the heel is placed on the near side. This will mean that the amount of pull from the foot is limited when rocking over, however it ensures that the heel has a good placement on the hold when the body is positioned over the foot and the weight pushes down onto it. As the climber rocks over his foot, the remaining push from the hand is limited and once sitting on his foot, he can reach for the next hold with ease and in complete control.

Dynamic Moves (Dynos).

Love them or hate them, sometimes you just can't reach the hold without a little (or a large) jump. The opposite of static moves, where the move is executed in a slow, controlled manner, dynamic moves are made in one rapid push. It is possible that static moves can be reversed, so if the reach is too far, you can back off from any point of the move. Dynamic moves rely on a powerful, explosive start allowing the momentum to carry you to the next hold. It is like bowling a heavy bowling ball. There is a point were even if you try and stop, too much momentum has been generated and the ball will be loosed no matter what. If we try and stop the bowl we are much more likely to almost drop the ball with less power and accuracy than if we committed. Dynos are more scary than bowling because if we miss, we will fall, but the principle is the same. Commit to the move and there is much more chance of success. Back out, and you are very likely to fall anyway. The following exercises should provide you with the skills needed to climb in a dynamic style if you need to.

Caution.

Whenever we make moves quickly and dynamically, our bodies take a pounding. When slapping for holds, even large jugs, the skin on our hands is likely to get blistered, calloused and ripped. This is likely to be exaggerated if we catch the hold, but cannot control the swing and our hand slips off. The joints, tendons and ligaments in the fingers, arms and especially the shoulders are likely to take heavy wear. Prior to undertaking Dynos, you should have warmed up thoroughly, and if you have shoulder injuries, treat them with great caution.

Lastly, spot your landing zone (especially if bouldering) unless you make the move first time, you will fall off. Ensure the area is adequately protected so you reduce the risk of injury to you and someone else. If you are able to, get spotted as this will reduce your chance of injury.

Coaching:

When coaching any form of dynamic move from slaps to full dynos, we need to be aware that climbers are likely to be nervous about falling. We should also pay particular attention to the caution above relating to injury.

It is helpful to start coaching these skills close to the floor to make the prospect of a fall less daunting.

Regarding setting up and the execution of the dynamic move, this is comprehensively covered below, and can be coached as described.

The main aspect for the climber to master is confidence in completing the move. To undertake this, there are three ways the climber can gain confidence to make a dynamic move without support.

- Whenever starting dynamic training, start with large holds and moves. Progress should be taken reasonably slowly as one bad fall can drastically affect and knock a climbers confidence.

- Hanging the target holds. The climber can be confident the holds are sufficiently positive to catch.
- Providing support during the push until the target hold is latched. When spotting climbers it can be common to place a hand into the small of the climbers back. This provides reassurance and slight support so the climber attempts the moves. When coaching dynos, this level of support can be increased as is required. When coaching younger climbers, it may be possible to provide a high level of support. Providing a "boost" and guiding them to the hold so it is easier to catch can make them feel the move is makeable. This level of support can be gradually reduced until the climber is able to make the move independently. When coaching adults, the amount of physical support provided to them can be limited, however it is still possible to guide the climber to the hold and reduce the chance that they will fall awkwardly.

Start Small, Learn to Slap.

Because we generally learn to climb in a controlled style, many people find it very difficult to overcome the fear of falling to be able to commit to dynamic moves. To get more used to more dynamic movements, start on a route that you have easily climbed before (preferably one with many jugs.) Rather than undertaking the moves in controlled movements, undertake each move quickly, as if it is a dyno. Each move, the hand slaps onto the next hold as the weight is pushed up the wall by the feet. You should attempt to release the hand when you are at the height of the push, then move the hand quickly as your momentum remains in the same place. Imagine throwing a ball in the air. There is a split second where it hovers, weightless. You should be snatching your hand up the wall during this brief weightless period. While it is not necessary to undertake the climb in this way, it will get you more used to this feeling of pushing and catching.

Your feet should remain on the holds, it is likely that your holding hand will remain on the hold (especially to start off with). If you are not keen on making quick movements or passing the point of no return, this exercise should expose and desensitize you to this feeling of insecurity. The distance between holds can be increased as your confidence grows. You have learned to slap for holds. As well as being upwards slaps, it is common to have to slap out to the side. This time, you should pull in with the hands to create the brief weightless state, and slap the hand out to the side when this is created.

Jumps.

Once you are comfortable slapping for holds around your full stretch, to gain further height, a jump will be needed to reach the target hold. The only alternative is to place your feet onto higher holds for the move to be made statically. Static moves where the hands and feet are close together are very strenuous and, in some cases a jump to the next hold may be more efficient. When jumping, your feet will come off the footholds. One hand will move to the target hold however one remaining hand stays on the lower hand hold. This move is between a slap and a full Dyno. The following steps introduce jumps.

Setting Up:

1. Identify the starting holds for the hands and feet and the target hold you will be jumping for.
2. Climb up using anything to hang the target hand holds. These will be the start hand hold and the higher target hold. This will identify the dead hang point and the correct position to attempt to catch the hold. Hang off the two handholds, taking your feet off the holds so you know the position you will need to jump into. First undertake this statically, taking the feet off slowly with no swing. This is the position you will be attempting to land in. Unless you are jumping straight up, there will be a swing from the legs which you will need to control. To practise this, place your hands on the finish handholds. Place your feet above / as close as you can to the footholds you use to start the jump. Take them off quickly and you will feel a swing similar to what you will experience when undertaking the jump for real. This may take a couple of trials to get comfortable with, and undertake while in control.
3. Now you are ready to attempt the jump.
4. Hang down off the handholds so the arms are straight and the legs are bent allowing for a powerful push. In this position, you are like a coiled spring ready to push to the next hold.
5. Your feet can be either both inside edge with the hips parallel to the wall, or twisted with an outside edge of the same foot to the hand which will move to the hold. Depending on the angle of the wall an inside or outside edge could feel preferable. Try both and determine personal preference. Twisting on the move may feel easier to undertake the initial push with the feet because twisting will keep your body closer in to the wall. However, because you will be closer to the wall, the swing (once the target holds are caught) will be greater. Having the hips parallel to the wall may make the push more strenuous on the arms, however it may make catching the target holds and controlling the swing easier. You may need to adapt your approach as the wall dictates, especially on larger overhangs where the swing will be harder to control.Personally, I prefer outside edge where possible because the twist brings your body into the wall and less inward pull with the arms is required.
6. When your legs have pushed you fully, you will experience a brief moment of weightlessness detailed above. Aim to catch the target hold in this brief moment before gravity starts pulling you back down again.
7. As soon as possible, place your feet back onto the next holds to remove weight from the arms.

Trajectory Considerations.

Our trajectory will be affected by gravity whenever we push and let go of the wall. When we are new to jumping, it does not occur to us that we will do anything apart from float in a straight line from where we have pushed, to where we want to finish. Physics has its own set of rules of which we are no exception. We need to consider our trajectory if we want to end in the right place to be able to catch the holds we are aiming for.

Think of throwing a ball for someone else to catch. If we aim our throw directly at their catching hand. The ball, affected by gravity will be pulled down, underneath their catching hand. The further the throw, the more gravity affects the ball and the lower it will fall below the target. To hit the target, we need to counteract this and aim the ball above the catching hand relative to the amount which it will be pulled down. Correctly undertaking this will result in a successful throw and catch. The same principle is applied if we throw a ball upwards, say to a friend on a balcony. Gravity affects the ball, and we need to aim above the balcony if we want it to end up there. Undertaking a jump or Dyno on an overhang utilises the same principle. Rather than aiming our push directly at the hold, we need to aim above it or closer into the wall. This will feel like we will push ourselves into the wall. In practise we will arc out allowing us to settle onto the target hold at the deadpoint we need to catch the hold.

When setting up, look at the hold, consider the trajectory and pick a spot on the wall to aim at. This spot will be between you and the target hold. Probably 25 - 50 cm closer to you than the hold, however where to aim depends on the angle of the wall and the distance you need to jump. Once this has been undertaken look away from the target hold to where you are aiming. While this sounds odd, continuing to look at the target hold will warp your trajectory and is likely to send you out, and too far away from the hold to catch it. Once you have pushed off with your feet, you can look for the target hold you intend to catch. You may think that this will not give you sufficient time to look for and catch the target hold in the air, however you are much more likely to stick the dyno if your centre of gravity is travelling correctly rather than trying to control a large swing or a jump too low.

Your arms, rather than attempting to pull you directly towards the hold will try to stabilize you and provide the aim rather than the power. Consider that when on a vertical wall your feet cannot push directly up the wall without your hands pulling you in, and when on an overhang, gravity will pull you down, away from the target hold.

When driving with your legs, you will be pushed out, away from the wall. Your arms therefore need to pull into the wall so the correct trajectory will be followed as discussed above. Again, it will feel like you will push yourself straight into the wall, however pulling in will give you the best chance of catching the target hold successfully. If you do not undertake this, you will push your centre of gravity to either too far below or far away from the wall to catch the hold. In the photo below, we can see that the climber is looking at the hold. As a result they have failed to consider their trajectory and they will push too far away from the hold to be able to catch it.

Catching the Target Hold:

When we jump, there will be a brief period where we are weightless. This will be at maximum height when the force of our push is equal to gravity pulling us down. The most efficient jump will mean that this point is exactly the height needed to catch the target hold. Just before we have reached this height, undertake a slap for the target hold so that your hands connect in this exact weightless moment. If the target hold is not directly above the launch holds, a swing will then need to be held. The further away the target hold, the larger the swing will be. The advantage of the jump, is if the lower hand is able to remain on the hold, it is able to provide a much greater element of control over the swing. This, combined with core strength and practise of controlling the swing prior to undertaking the jump, will provide the best chance of catching the target hold successfully.

The trajectory considerations discussed above also play a large part in how easy it will be to catch and remain on the target handhold, especially when undertaking full dynamic moves where both hands and feet leave the holds.

If we jump too short (or have not committed to the move), our centre of gravity does not reach the deadpoint underneath the target hold. In this circumstance we have to control and hold a larger swing as the body pendulums under the target hold. It is common that the swing is too much to control, the climber lets go and falls flat on their face.

If, on the other hand we jump too far, the momentum created by the jump will carry on past the hold. This will make catching the target hold very hard, as the body continues to travel past the optimum direction of pull of the target hold. This can aptly be illustrated when the climber desperately claws at the air in an attempt to pull themselves back to the hold they have gone sailing past, often landing flat on their back. In the rare circumstance that the climber manages to catch the hold, because the centre of gravity has passed the target hold, the climber has to catch the hold in a poor direction of pull. In all but a few cases this requires too much strength to control and again the climber falls off.

Aiming in between these two points; for your jump to settle your centre of gravity on to the deadhang point will make the catch the easiest to tame. The diagram below shows how the differences of where we aim to jump to, can drastically affect how much swing we have when we catch the target handhold(s).

Jumping:

- Drive with the legs.
- Pull (in) with the arms.
- When your feet start to leave the foot holds, look for the handhold.
- Raise the hand to catch the target hold.
- Control the swing.
- Place your feet on to the next holds to get stable and balanced.

Full Dynamic Moves.

Once you have mastered jumps, it is time to take on a full dynamic move. This is similar to a large jump, however when we drive up, the distance between the start and target holds is so great that both hands and both feet leave the starting holds. If you have practised and are confident undertaking jumps, there should not be much more of an extension from jumps to Dynos. The trajectory considerations however are even more important as you will completely let go of the wall and cannot control yourself in the air. If you find that you are missing the target hold(s), pay more attention to your trajectory and adjust as required. With some Dynos, you will catch the holds with both hands and some you will only catch with one. You will almost certainly have a favoured hand. Like any of the skills contained within this book, you should practise until you are proficient with both your strong and weaker hand. Video 19 contains clips of successful and unsuccessful dynos.

Skills

Advanced Route Reading

Following on from route reading covered in section 1, you should already be able to identify the handholds, footholds and where your centre of gravity will be to use them efficiently. On easier climbs, you are likely to be able to flow, move to move from the start of a route to the end. What happens when we move onto harder routes with weird sequences or moves that stop you in your tracks?

Some routes have a definite hard part or crux. With the skills we have already put into practise, we should be able to plan below and above the crux move(s). Rather than just jumping on and having a go, which is likely to result in time being taken to figure out the moves at the crux, relook at the hard section a number of times. If possible, from a couple of angles. It is not cheating to climb an adjacent route to look at the holds (although it is to swing across and have a practise if we want to flash it first go!)

One very helpful skill to learn is what is a comfortable distance between your hands and your feet. This is a very difficult skill to learn. The simple reason for this is that your hands and feet can be very close to each other, or at your full stretch. This gives a huge variance of where your feet could be on the wall when your hands are on specific holds. The best way of learning and applying this is to discuss with your belayer after the climb and get them to take note of which holds your feet use in relation to your hands. Another tip is to video your climb so you can see for yourself. The more you can pay attention to what is a comfortable height for your feet and what it too high / low to use, the easier planning your footwork selection becomes.

We will consider how to read two particular problems:

- Stopper moves / holds.
- Technical / confusing sequences.

Stopper moves are fairly straight forward. You will find a move, or section which looks particularly hard. This could be strengthy, jumpy or technical. Using the skills listed in Sets one to three, consider what move would likely be most effective to get you past the specific move. It is common to feel foxed, however have a plan of at least two different ways in which you could pass this point. Once you reach this section, you will have a number of possible solutions to the problem. It may be that once on the crux holds, it feels like it will lend itself to a certain style. If this is the case, go with it and continue climbing. If this was the same way you read the route. Good. If your plan was not the way you managed it, or if you were unable to pass the crux section, ask yourself some questions:

- Was the way I climbed it an efficient way of making it past the move?
- If I try again, would I be able to climb it the way I planned?
- Would another technique have been more effective?

Remember the outcome and apply it to future climbs if a similar move appears again.

With stopper holds, the angle the we can use them is much smaller. In cases where we encounter routes with definite stopper holds, carefully consider where your centre of gravity needs to be to use the hold the most effectively. Next consider whether it is possible to put into practise any of the techniques to make the hand hold feel less insecure. Again have a couple of possibilities to try before you get to the hold so that you can have a good attempt.

With confusing sequences, if you are finding that you are route reading and getting wrong handed, start from a hold which must be a certain hand hold and work back to the beginning of the sequence. This will provide you with the sequence of hands which must be in certain positions or on certain holds. Run through the sequence a couple of times to ensure that you remember it. When you approach the start, recall the plan and ensure that you stick to it. Sometimes it helps to talk yourself through the problem. "That hold needs to be left hand... so the hold below must be a right hand, and the one below that is a left hand again." Talk your plan through with your spotter / belayer. If you start the sequence with the wrong hand, they can always shout and correct you.

Coaching:

Route reading as a skill can be particularly hard for people to undertake. The simple way to get better is to practise and reflect on how close to the plan the climb was executed. Many climbers question the practise and relevance of route reading, especially as they state that they are not able to remember the whole route as soon as they start climbing. Part of this has been covered in the initial route reading section. The climber is indeed unlikely to be able to remember the whole of the route, however when they get to the crux section, as long as they have made a plan, they will spend less time considering the route while actually climbing it. It should be simple to explain that planning while standing on the floor is significantly easier than planning while hanging on to the wall.

Recording the climber reading, then climbing the route can provide valuable, structured feedback about the plan they made in comparison to the way in which they climbed the route. They will be able to consider where the plan was incorrect, and what they are capable of compared to what they think they are capable of. Visualisation of exactly how to climb a route, knowing exactly where the climbers hands and feet will be is an immensely difficult skill, but is imperative to reach a climbers on sight potential.

Appropriate Twisting on a Route.

After we have learned any new skill, or bought any new toy, it is natural that we want to play with it as much as possible. In terms of climbing however the styles taught in Sets one and two; rock over's and twisting may be interchangeable depending on the route climbed. Which style you decide to use will depend on a number of things, including how you feel on the day! So how do we decide when to stay hips square onto the wall and when to twist? The short answer is experience. The more you know your body and the types of moves you are able to undertake with each technique, you can decide what to use and when. There are a couple of things to bear in mind:

- Inside edge rockovers are mainly beneficial on slabs.
- Twisting and pivoting is most appropriate on overhangs.
- Vertical walls are interchangeable between the two styles however twisting may be more beneficial for resting and climbers with less bicep and shoulder strength.
- The more pronounced the slab / overhang, the more likely each technique is at being effective.

When learning whether it is more appropriate to twist or to use a rock over, filming your climbs is a very good way of determining how hard you are working. Remember when we are learning skills, we should drop the difficulty down a couple of grades from our limit. When climbing harder problems, film the climb first time you attempt it. Expect that there will be some moves which feel hard and like your efficiency could be improved. When you work the moves and attempt differing straight v bent arm moves, film subsequent attempts. You should be able to compare which looks and feels easier. When you have determined the easiest way to climb it, film the attempt again. Comparing the before and after footage should provide you with a route which looks and feels efficient. If it looks efficient, it probably is. This is the hardest section to master because you are comparing subtle differences in your climbing style, trying to find the most efficient way of climbing.

Finding and Using Rests and Clipping Positions When Leading.

You already know what position a rest will be for: rock overs, twisting rest position, bridging and utilising volumes, heel / toe hooking corners. All of these give us a break for the arms to recover before pushing onto the next part of the climb. We may also be able to gain partial rests when a large "thank god" jug presents on a hard route.

Full Rests.

A full rest is where we are able to take both hands off the wall at the same time (or at least only be holding very loosely with one.) When we get the opportunity to have a full rest, unless you have a pressing appointment later, take your time to actually have a full rest. This is likely to be for minutes rather than seconds. However when bouldering or climbing indoor, it is normally intended that the climb should be completed in a single push without stopping to rest. Boulder and roped routes are therefore likely to be set with minimal if any full rest positions. With that said, if you find a full rest spot, and need to recover for a couple of minutes before climbing to the top, your route will still count as a successful ascent. If you sit on the rope to take your rest this isn't allowed (in competition at least!)

When resting, more weight will be transferred to your feet and legs. There are times when we start to climb on, not because our arms have recovered, but because our legs are starting to feel a little shaky. Before you climb on, consider whether you regained enough arm strength to climb to the top. If not, consider repositioning to a more comfortable position.

Partial Rests.

Good hand holds can give us enough time to have a brief rest, shake out a tired arm, maybe chalk up and then continue climbing. Because the rest requires another hand to be holding on, (albeit on a larger hold) this is more strenuous than the full rest. We are likely to recharge one arm, while strength is draining out of the other. Depending on how strenuous a position we are in, it may be possible that we are draining energy from the holding arm more quickly than we are regaining it from the resting one. On some routes, close to the top, where we just need to recharge a bit before completing the climb, this may be useful. However lower down, will taking this rest solve the problem or just make both arms tired? Either way, partial rests can be useful, but we need to keep in mind how much energy we are using and whether we will be able to complete the route if we rest for too long.

Endurance training will improve the amount of time you can hang on, with any training however this should not be at the expense of finding and using adequate rest positions. It may mean that you can power through routes of a moderate grade, however when taking on harder climbs, you are unlikely to have the endurance to complete this in one push and you will be less likely to identify rest points having not developed this skill on previous climbs. If you are seeking to transfer to outdoor climbing, training for 10 – 15 Meter indoor routes will bear little resemblance to the endurance required for longer outdoor routes. It is likely that powering through indoor climbs without resting will hinder your ability on longer outdoor routes. To train for longer climbs, consider undertaking endurance training alongside finding and utilising rest spots where possible.

For a vertical or overhanging walls, the rest position should be off a good hold on a straight arm. It is likely to be with a twisted position but again bear in mind, the more we lean back, the more energy will be draining from the holding arm. Remember the heel rock over and see if this provides an adequate rest position.

Clipping Positions.

Clipping efficiently is an important skill to consider when leading. When we look at people clipping, especially those quite new to leading, there is a tendency to clip the next quickdraw high above them, as soon as it can be reached. This is generally because people push their comfort zone while leading and to make them feel slightly more secure, they clip as soon as possible. There are a number of things to consider to determine the optimum clipping position.

- The higher the clip, the longer it is likely to take to clip it.
- The more rope that is paid out, the further we would fall.
- Could the clip be built into a move?

High v Low Clipping Positions.

Clipping high, as far as we can reach can have some advantages. However clipping low can be equally effective. So what is best? It is difficult to answer this question, because rather than basic climbing safety which can be quite black and white, the answers here are more shades of grey.

The most basic thing to weigh up is the higher you attempt to clip, the more rope that is in the system. Therefore the further you will fall if you do come off. The lower the clip, the less rope in the system and the smaller the fall would be.

The second thing to consider is how positive are the holds which we will be using to clip from? If you would not use the holds for a partial rest, it is probably best not to attempt to clip from them. Clipping is likely to only take a matter of seconds, however it is very common to see climbers attempting to clip on holds they can barely stay on because they want to "get safe". To clip off small holds increases your tension level as well as having a higher chance of falling, you are also more likely to fumble the clip due to your increased stress level.

The third and final consideration is what are the holds like around you? If you are on positive holds, with the crux coming up, you may wish to reach and clip high protecting the hard move(s). On the other hand, if you have already passed the crux and the remaining holds are positive, clipping above you will take extra time and may not be the most effective thing to do. In situations like this, you will need to be aware whether you favour high clips because of stress. If you do, train yourself to be comfortable getting a little higher before reaching a more efficient clipping position. This is covered in the section on falling below.

Considering these factors should provide you with a positive clipping position. When you read the route you are about to lead, you should be looking for both clipping and rest positions. Have a favoured position and an alternate, in case you get to that point and find it more difficult than expected.

There may even be times where you are between clips that you have not yet clipped, a low one at the waist and a higher one above you. Rather than dropping the rope, it is sometimes possible to clip two or extremely even three clips in one go. This takes slightly longer than a single clip, however saves a tremendous amount of time and energy overall. It can however only be undertaken where the holds are positive enough to spend the extended period of time hanging off one hand while clipping. Video 20 views various differing clipping options while climbing the same route on a wall.

Building Clipping into Moves.

Clipping is strenuous. Reaching down, grabbing your rope, pulling it to the clip, clipping and then replacing your hand onto the hold all takes time and energy. This is time that will get you very tired, very quickly. The most efficient climbers, where possible, clip in as they are making the next move. The time it takes to clip is built into the move and progress on the route is maintained. Where possible, look for clips that are in between holds the hand will pass. Grab the rope while in the resting position. While making the move, as the hand passes the quickdraw, clip in the rope then place the hand onto the next hold. This works much better with a twisting stance as it is much less strenuous, however equally, it can be done with a more strenuous rock over. Video 21 looks at the differing clipping principles on the same route.

Resting on lead routes is the same principal as it is on any other, however there is another trick we can use when climbing right at our limit. We have discussed above that clipping takes time and energy. In extreme cases, some people miss clips to save energy. This is usually done by the top climbers when working their projects outdoors. Do not undertake this indoor or the friendly floor walkers will be "having a chat with you" about clipping policies. So instead of missing clips, what we can do is climb the start of a route, say half way, then climb back down leaving the rope in place. You can then have a full rest on the floor and when recovered, cruise back up your high point having saved a lot of energy on the lower section. This counts as a successful ascent so long as you do not weight the rope, and are able to reverse the start moves without falling. Again a note on this, if the wall you are climbing is particularly overhanging, if you fall off with the top rope in place it is likely to result in a large swing. If this is the case, you may wish to check with the centre before using this type of tactic on an overhanging route.

Appropriate Use of Speed on a Climb.

Any time spent holding onto a wall, uses energy. The less time we are climbing, the less tired we will become. To illustrate this, climb a route (to start off with a relatively easy one) at a slow pace. The wall should be at least vertical, preferably, slightly overhanging. You should be able to make perfect foot placements and concentrate on getting your balance in the correct position. Consider how much energy you have used. Climb the route again, each time increasing your pace. It is suggested that you increase speed by roughly 20%, taking time to rest in between attempts. This will enable you to try and climb fast while still remaining controlled in your movements. When your technique begins to suffer, and you start to make mistakes, climb slightly slower so that overall pace is increased, but your technique remains good and efficient. Note the difference in time between the first slow attempt and your fastest, but still efficient climb. Consider how strenuous each climb felt. You should feel that you have expended less energy if your technique remains the same but you spend less time on the route.

Having undertaken this on an easy wall, try something a bit more challenging. As routes get harder, there are likely to be more pronounced cruxes / difficult stages. We should climb these harder sections at the pace we need to complete them successfully. This is likely to be slower than we were climbing before. Once the hard section has been passed, we can again speed up. The result should be that because we climb faster on the easier sections, we may have saved sufficient energy to successfully complete the route.

Dealing With Fear.

Fear and our comfort zone keeps us safe. Without it we wouldn't live very long. From an early age, we learn to respect consequences and pain is a good motivating factor to not repeat the same mistakes. With that said, we undertake a variety of pretty risky behaviours every day. Alcohol and tobacco cause harm. We all know this. However the effects are usually not immediate and we are very good at blocking future effects from our mind even though they are exceedingly likely to occur. Smoking is probably the most risky, damaging activity that we can undertake for a lengthy period of time. However we are not scared of a cigarette. If the effect was instant and we knew one cigarette would kill us, we wouldn't go near them and they would be banned.

Consider some other risk factors from the list below:

- Cycling in cities.
- Playing with venomous snakes.
- Motorway driving.
- Surfing with sharks.
- Driving Death Road in Bolivia.
- Being driven along Death Road as a passenger.
- Playing with a friends German Shepherd / Staffordshire Bull Terrier.
- Playing Russian Roulette.
- Flying.
- BASE Jumping (parachuting off a cliff, bridge, building or antenna).

Put these into a list of how scared they would make you feel. Order them from the most scary at the top and the least scary at the bottom. Each person will have a personalised list and there is no right or wrong answer.

1 – Most Scary	
2	
3	
4	
5	
6	
7	
8	
9	
10 – Least Scary	

Where would you insert different styles of climbing into the list? Think about top roping, leading, auto belays and bouldering? Assume the climb is at your limit and you are quite likely to fall.

When we consider risk assessments, which you have just undertaken, we rank activities from a detached view. Formal risk assessments consider the probability of a bad effect happening against the severity of what the effect would be. When we undertake our own risk assessments, we also consider our own fears and comfort zones which drastically affect our consideration of the risk. While all of the activities on the list are possibly fatal, most people put cycling and driving towards the bottom of the list and add climbing as a more dangerous activity. Why? Control and Normality.

There is likely to be a large element of control clouding your answers. Generally, we feel in control in our cars. We feel like we can steer out of danger on our bikes. We feel less in control whilst on an airplane which is one reason why many more people are nervous of flying. However how much are we actually in control of?

Ask any biker whether accidents are caused by their riding or by other motorists. The majority have confidence in their riding ability believing that it is other road users who don't see them and cause the accidents. Which statement did you put first regarding driving v being driven along death road?

Considering mechanical failure, do we have sufficient knowledge to maintain our vehicles and know for certain that they will not break and crash? No, we put our faith in the manufacturers to build a sturdy product and the mechanics who maintain and service our vehicles keeping them safe and road worthy. Mechanical failure is most people's main concern, however accidents occur rarely because of this... it is almost always human error. However illogically we still feel in control when we are driving.

Now compare driving to the auto belays which most people find pretty scary, especially to start with. Auto belays are carefully designed, tested, and once in use, serviced regularly. Many still find them scary because we do not have another human on the other end. Considering human error is by far the lead cause of accidents, and our safety controls are limited to correctly fitting a harness and clipping in, why is it so scary for the majority of people? Comparing mechanical error, there is probably very little difference in the chance of either a car or an auto belay malfunctioning. However many still find using auto belays to be more scary.

Next, let us compare the result of a potential accident. A fall from the top of a 10 Meter wall, if a total failure occurs to the belayer / auto belay, the climber will hit the floor at just under 30 miles per hour. This is likely to result in broken bones or maybe worse, depending on the landing. However equally, we could escape with minor injuries. Now consider the result if your engine seizes and your car suddenly loses control at 70+ miles per hour. The most probable result is very serious injury, likely worse. The car still feels safer to many people even though if there is a total malfunction, there is a much greater chance of a serious life changing (or ending) incident occurring.

So comparing climbing with driving and having looked at the risks, the effects and the lack of control we have over the situations, when they are both compared, generally people still find climbing more risky.

The cause of this is desensitisation. We become accustomed to risks which have potentially severe consequences because they are the norm. Consider the difference between the examples provided at the beginning. We are at serious risk from playing with venomous snakes and surfing with sharks in the same way that we are from being attacked by a dog. However, we are accustomed to having dogs as pets, and we feel that we can control dogs, so having them as pets feels safe. Especially for children the outcome of an attack from the above examples is likely to be similar, very serious injury or death.

When we climb with ropes we give our complete safety to the belayer and trust that they will prevent us from hitting the floor. Even though the belayer is in complete control of our safety, we still have some element of control, because we select who will belay for us. It needs to be accepted that you can only control your climb and must trust your belayer to catch you if you fall and lower you down safely. Some people find this easier than others, and when we start climbing many people get nervous reaching the top of the wall. Similarly we get nervous on the way down, especially if the belayer lets us down fast or in a jerky manner. After a few months though, this fear dissipates and we tend to only get nervous when changing belay partner or on a route when we are likely to take a fall. In short, climbing for a few months starts to desensitise us from the height and enables us to trust the belayer. Now we need to conquer the fear of falling.

Falling like any other fear can be overcome. We just need to be desensitised to climb your hardest and not worry about taking a fall. We discussed having our normal comfort zone at the beginning of this section. All actions we undertake can be placed into our comfort zone. Certain activities are towards the centre and are very easy for us to undertake. Other more daunting tasks can be placed towards the edge or just outside our comfort zone, which we have the ability to undertake but are scary. Lastly we have things well outside our comfort zone which are too scary for us to carry out.

Consider your comfort zone, and decide where the following statements fit into the table:

Situation.	Comfort Zone		
	Centre	Edge	Way out
Easy climb on a vertical wall.			
Easy climb on an overhang.			
Being lowered down a route.			
Jumping off an auto belay.			
Being lower by the auto belay.			
Slapping for holds (you are not sure you will hold on to.)			
Climbing with a slack top rope.			
Top rope while fatigued, fingers barely able to grip, unfurling.			
Jumping off a top rope.			
Having an uncontrolled fall due to fatigue while on a top rope.			
Jumping off while on lead.			
Slapping for holds while on lead.			
Climbing above your last clip.			
Leading while completely fatigued, fingers unfurling.			
Bouldering an easy slab.			
Bouldering a hard slab where you are likely to slip.			
Climbing high on a boulder.			
Climbing high on a boulder with poor holds and large moves.			
Needing to dyno for the top hold on a high boulder problem.			

Your comfort zone is malleable. Think of how much larger it has got and how much more you are able to do since you started climbing. There are a couple of ways the range of your comfort zone can be expanded:

- Kill or Cure - all at once immersion OR
- Little by little, systematic desensitisation.

Think about gambling for a second. Pretty much everything we do in life is a gamble. Relationships, changing jobs, committing time to training. Everything has its own reward and consequence if it goes wrong. Considering fear training again, it is a gamble. Consider your comfort zone is a pile of ten chips. If you win, you get your chips back and half as much again. Kill or cure training costs eight chips, systematic desensitisation costs two chips. The odds of winning are the same. What would you bet?

Kill or cure training works with a select few people. While you may take large lead falls, if you are not ready for this style of training, even if you don't get hurt, it is likely to be so scary that overall it is a negative experience. If this is the case, you have lost most of your chips and your comfort zone reduces dramatically. Consider being scared of leading and chucking yourself onto a hard route with difficult moves where you are likely to take a fall. Even if you get to the top, it is likely that the route will have scared you so much that you won't want to do another and you are put off lead climbing altogether. Therefore the odds of kill or cure training working are actually lower. Would you still risk a large pile of chips for an outside bet to increase your comfort zone quicker? Most people would not.

In terms of falling training and overcoming this fear, it is recommended that you take things slowly for a lower risk, smoother gain. Systematic desensitisation is therefore the preferred style of training for the majority of people.

Another thing to note, consider that if you do not place any bets the value of your chips does not increase as no interest is paid. Due to inflation, your chips are worth less over time than they were when you first had them. Staying within your comfort zone, will slowly reduce it over time. Just avoiding things which we are afraid of will lead to additional anxiety when we come to work on them later. Staying still is like moving backwards.

Using the previous examples, plot where you are on the scale and order each situation into descending order of fear. This way, the least scary things should be at the top and the most scary at the bottom. You will know which situations are comfortable for you and which situations you avoid. Feel free to add more to your list if there are some others personal to you. Split the situations into bouldering, top ropes and leading. You should end up with an example like this on the page below:

Boulder	Top Rope	Lead
Easy traversing.	Easy climb.	Easy climb on the slab.
Easy ascending, large holds.	Feeling the rope tight all the time.	Clipping above your head.
Easy moves, smaller holds.	Slapping for holds.	Taking small controlled jumps.
Leaning off arms when high on the wall (good holds).	Having the rope loose on the top rope (30 cm slack).	Slapping for holds.
Slapping for holds.	Taking small top rope falls.	Climbing with more difficult moves / holds.
High up Dynos.	Climbing when pumped.	Climbing above the last clip.
Moves at your limit when high up and arms are pumped.	Taking uncontrolled falls.	Taking uncontrolled falls.

The table above is just for illustration. There are likely to be many more factors for each of the styles of climbing which you can order into your list of comfort. At this stage, focus on the situations on the edge of your comfort zone, as discussed these do not want to be too far outside to prevent backwards progress. The following exercises can be adapted as needed and will work at breaking down your barriers and allowing you to make progress.

Here are some techniques to deal with fear and regain your composure that cut across all types of climbing.

Breathing.

Breathing keeps us alive. It also provides us with the oxygen we need to make energy. While some sports - 100 Meter sprint for example can be undertaken without breathing, longer exertions can not. We need to breathe to maintain our energy for climbing further. It is as simple as that! Have you ever found that after hard sequences you have been panting? It is likely that you have been concentrating so much on the route that your breathing has been affected. Either it has stopped completely, or has been so shallow and rapid that it is ineffective. When getting to hard or scary sections, after you have made a move, force yourself to take a breath. While this may take a second or two, it is better than trying to climb while choking yourself.

As well as providing us with energy, breathing makes us calm. It is one of the bodies most primitive urges. Imagine having your head held under water or having an Asthma attack. I am sure many of us have been "ducked" in a pool as kids. Panic and struggling, clawing to get a breath. If we hold our breath while making hard moves, we feel scared over the moves and because we are not breathing the problem is compounded. By comparison, look at any relaxation book or website. Breathing will feature heavily and is probably the first topic covered. After you have read the route, tied on or sat down for the sit start, close your eyes, breathe. Give your hands a little shake so your forearms are loose and start to climb. As you climb, you should continue to listen to your breathing ensuring that you are fully breathing in and out. Try and keep this under control in reasonably even breaths, not panting or gulping. The more scary the route becomes, continuing to concentrate on breathing will reduce the anxiety while keeping your energy levels up.

Finding Positions to Shake Out.

Getting scared makes us tense up. Tensing up makes us grip the holds harder. Harder than we need to. This makes the moves feel more strenuous and the climb more physical than it needs to be. We therefore get more tense. This vicious circle makes us over-grip holds leading to exhaustion and ultimately failing on / falling off the route. The only way to break this cycle is to calm down and relax. Just breathing doesn't make our muscles less tense, and we continue to over-grip holds, so the cycle continues. If you have realised that you are over-gripping holds, you need to find a rest so you are able to take either or both hands off the wall, in most cases one at a time. Take a second to breathe as you shake your arms out. Loosening the muscles in the forearm as you breathe steadily releases both the stress level as well as the muscle tension. When you replace your hand on the hold it is likely to feel much better than before. Aim to gently rest your hand on the hold when you replace it and this will assist. The effect of this rest is that you will be slightly more energised and less stressed. As you are now relaxed, you can return to efficient climbing rather than having a vice like grip.

A very simple example of the effectiveness of this, is people who are new to top roping tend to grip the knot or rope very tightly when they are being lowered off. You will see this with their white knuckle ride to the floor. Just getting them to close their eyes and breathe does not work as they are still tense in their arms and they remain very anxious. If they are able to let go for a few seconds, close their eyes, breathe and then gently replace their hands on the rope; this does work, and they feel less stressed and safer. They are still leaning back on the rope. They are still being lowered to the floor, so the situation is the same, but they feel better.

Distraction.

Some people like a simple distraction, some people hate it. Climbing with earphones and music can be a good way to distract yourself from everything else in the centre / crag. I would suggest that these are small with the wires tucked away to avoid snagging issues. Climbing walls are noisy, busy places and in some cases hearing everything else around you is a huge distraction from your climbing. Sticking earphones in can have a number of advantages **if it works for you**:

You concentrate only on your climb. Other noise is blocked out, and whereas we might have paused to take a look round, without earphones in we continue to climb. This can be other climbers in the centre falling, grunting, or people watching you and commenting on your climb. This can be particularly off putting and while some people revel in being watched, others find it so off-putting that they are unable to climb properly.

Also when you have earphones in something strange happens. While we are pumping sound in, we can hear our own breathing more. Earphones allow you more effectively to monitor your breathing with the benefits of this covered above.

Of course utilising this technique will cease your ability to communicate with your belay partner, so you will need to weigh up the pros and the cons of climbing with earphones to determine whether this technique is of benefit to you.

Increasing Bouldering Confidence.

Note* With Bouldering I never recommend that climbers take repeated jumps. The simple reason for this is that there are vastly more accidents recorded in bouldering areas compared to the roped areas. By repeatedly jumping down, even if you land on your feet each time, you are risking a bad landing... and it only takes one to pick up a horrible injury. So do not practise jumping from the top and expect that this "training" will end well.

Leaning Off Arms When High on the Wall.

Leaning back off your arms when you are high up is understandably scary. To the unpractised it can feel like leaning off a barrier over a long drop. Due to using outside edge or flagging and keeping the arms straight, if your hand slips off the hold you will land flat on your back, or worse, neck or head. However it may be the most efficient, or only way to make the move. To get over this fear, there are a couple of ways in which we can analyse the some of the factors causing us fear:

- Leaning back, using the outside edge.
- Being high up.

If you practise specific moves and skills, for example leaning back off your arms, you will become more and more comfortable undertaking these types of moves. This practise should be undertaken on a wall which is low and therefore if you fall, there is little chance of injury. You could also practise these moves with the safety of a top rope which will achieve the same effect, your confidence using this type of move brings them towards the middle of your comfort zone.

At the same time, you should also practise gaining greater exposure of height. This can be undertaken by repeated bouldering to the top on routes within your ability. Rather than just climbing straight down, spend some time at the top of the wall. Look around and take in the view (albeit just a cloud of chalk dust indoors). When you are confident at this, you could try a high level traverse. You should be able to use relatively easy holds as the finishing holds to many boulder problems are fairly large. Ensure there is no-one underneath you when you undertake this and it may not be possible if the wall is busy. This exposure of making reasonably safe moves continually at height should make you confident at being high up. You can increase this exposure by starting to make harder, but achievable moves at a greater height.

Once you are both confident in the moves and with climbing whilst being reasonably high up, you are ready to start attempting the moves which you previously thought were scary. Employ your best spotter and have a go. Breaking the fear into manageable chunks and practicing them until they are both within your comfort zone should make this feel easier.

Roped Climbing.

Similar to the bouldering example, if there are specific issues with types of moves that you are uncomfortable with; you should be able to determine what these moves are, and work to improve your confidence in making them.

Unless we get comfortable with falling, this primeval fear will limit us from climbing to our potential. So, we have practised the coping with fear techniques listed above and can remain calm on most routes, but falling can still be so scary that we refuse to risk it. We may grab another hold on a differing route, call for the rope to be taken in, anything apart from fall off. As discussed before, if we actively avoid falling, it will get further and further outside our comfort zone.

Top Ropes.

To start off with, just letting go at the top of the wall and transferring our weight to the rope can be an emotional experience. This does not mean that you are a nervous person, just that you have a healthy sense of consequence and respect for height. As people get more experienced, once the rope has been taken tight, we sit back quicker and quicker. This of course depends entirely on having a stable belayer whom we trust. The issue is that we trust a slack rope less and less. To gain more confidence at making hard moves and risking falls follow the training sets below.

Note * When undertaking any falling exercises you should consult with your belayer. They should be ready and expecting to hold falls. As they get more competent, this is likely to be less of an issue, however especially when starting out, let them know before the climb or session that they will be holding repeated falls, sometimes with no warning aside from your discussion before you start. The risks of an unexpected fall are obvious.

Start Small, Get Bigger.

Start on a vertical or slightly overhanging wall so that you will fall into space. Climb until you are half way up. Make sure that there are no volumes, large holds or other hazards beside or below you. The belayer should be ready to catch you. They will have to do nothing aside from hold the fall, so you should be able to trust them completely, but have them backed up if you wish. This will give you the confidence to undertake what is coming next. Take one step up. This will create roughly 30 - 60 cm of slack in the rope. With this amount of slack in the system take a small hop backwards. You will experience a small fall. You should attempt to take a jump backwards of roughly 30 cm. Let go with your hands! While this sounds basic, some people attempt to loosely leave a hand on the wall just in case. This is pointless as you won't be able to hold yourself and are just risking injury. A tip which helps is place one hand onto your knot, then hop back letting go with the other hand. When you jump, train yourself to raise your legs as if jumping into the lower off position. It is natural to want to put your feet to the floor. However the rope will catch you, so this is pointless. Also if you put your feet down to the floor, you will swing into the wall and land flat on your face. This is unpleasant and is unlikely to motivate you to try again, however keep practicing until you are able to jump with a small amount of slack straight into the lower off position. You should undertake this exercise until it no longer feels scary. Once it has become normal, climb to a higher point and repeat the exercise. The distance that you fall should remain the same. Repeat these small falls higher and higher up the wall until you are confident at taking a small fall at any height of the wall.

When you are happy with this, climb to roughly three quarters the way up the wall and undertake slightly larger falls, one larger step or two smaller steps up. This could generate up to a meter of slack in the rope, and again you will need to get used to taking a larger fall and your belayer will get used to holding it.

Once you are comfortable with taking reasonable sized planned falls, it is time to tackle unexpected falls.

Unplanned Top Rope Falls.

Unplanned falls seem more scary for two reasons, we do not know that our belayer will be able to catch us and we are less controlled in the air so we are worried about swinging back into the wall. To start off with agree with your belayer that you will be jumping on a specific route and you will not give them any notice. Again, they may wish to be backed up for the first few tries to ensure that they are also confident. When you have undertaken a few climbs jumping sporadically throughout, you should trust your belayer sufficiently to hold any fall.

Now you are ready to undertake uncontrolled falls. Climb routes around and above your limit. Avoid falling close to the floor, and if you need to, climb an easier route until you are around half way. Transfer onto the other harder route and start to make harder and harder moves, probably slapping for holds which feel poor. There should be no greater slack in the rope than when you started the original falling training, so you should only fall a similar distance as before. There are two things which will be trained in this exercise:

- Getting comfortable using smaller holds and making more tenuous, difficult moves.
- You will also be exposed to taking small but uncontrolled falls when you fail to make the hard moves you are attempting.

Using the same principle as the previous exercise, once you have gained confidence in taking unexpected falls, start to push higher up the wall, and increasing the amount of slack in the rope. Again, this should not exceed much more than a meter, after which you should have gained confidence climbing at your limit while risking and taking unexpected falls.

Falling as a Result of Muscle Failure.

The last exercise with a top rope is to fall as a result of exhaustion rather than letting go. Climbing with very little "gas left in the tank" exaggerates the fear of falling. We are desperately climbing on, knowing that we will fall, but we are somehow still climbing. We would much prefer to take a hop and at least end that feeling, but if we want to get the most out of ourselves, can we push another move? It can be very surprising what we are actually capable of. The only way to test this is to climb a route continually until muscle failure occurs. Choose a route of moderate difficulty, probably just below your comfortable on-sight grade. Climb the route again and again with no rest in between until you cannot hold on any more and your grip fails. Resist the temptation to control the feeling by jumping or grabbing larger holds and keep pushing until the fall eventually happens. Count the moves / whole climbs it took between getting the feeling that you can't hold on until you actually let go. This will improve a number of aspects. You will improve your endurance. You will take a properly uncontrolled fall. You will become more aware that feeling tired does not mean that you can't push through the last few moves and complete a route successfully.

Undertaking this type of training is hard both physically and mentally. I would suggest only undertaking it when both you and your belayer are confident. I would also only suggest undertaking it at the end of a session as you will be so tired afterwards that even after a reasonable rest, you will be unable to get any more effective climbing done.

Leading Specific Exercises.

This section does not cover any of the safety or skills associated with lead climbing. In no way is this intended to replace a lead climbing course where leading safety would be taught. If you require instruction in leading technique, clipping, belaying or other safety, book a lead course at your local centre. It is envisaged that if you are reading this section, you are a competent lead climber and are of sufficient experience to ensure your safety while undertaking the following exercises. These exercises are commonly used and safe if undertaken correctly. I accept no responsibility if you mess up and die.

Redpointing.

If you are a competent lead climber but are not confident to lead certain routes, you can consider seconding or undertaking "ghost" leads. This involves climbing secured by a top rope while clipping a lead rope to gain confidence on the route. Many leaders start this way while getting to grips with clipping and the stress level. Climbers of all abilities use the same procedures on projects and climbs before finally successfully climbing them. We call it Redpointing, and there is no difference in the grade. Practicing a 4 is the same principle as practicing an 8 or a 9, and if you need to practise the route to succeed, just do it. Climbing in this way allows you to not just work individual moves, but also get a feel for efficient clipping positions, and the overall endurance required for the route. Just seconding routes however and never taking falls does not reduce your fear of falling, and should be undertaken in conjunction with fall training so that you are confident to remove the top rope when you are ready.

Getting Above your Clip.

Leading suddenly feels scary when our eyes get higher than the clip. As soon as this happens, we can no longer see our safety rope above us and psychologically, this can be a big challenge. Consider climbers who look comfortable and smooth when they have a top rope, but whenever they get above their clip, their climbing seems jerky and timid. Their moves don't flow and they seem tense until they have clipped high again. The issue is that clipping high wastes energy and risks a larger fall. This is covered above in the clipping section. What we need to remember is that we still have a top rope until our knot is the same height as the quick draw. Many people seem to forget this, and as soon as their face passes the clip, they start to freak out. Don't. Look down and check. You will only experience fall similar to that of a top rope until your knot is above the clip. If you experience anxiety being above your clip, to progress, you need to get comfortable with it!

Start on easy, safe routes. When you reach the point that you can see above the clip, find a rest position and take a couple of seconds to just breathe and look around. Make a move up. Again, find a rest position and breathe. Repeat this until you can clip the next clip without reaching up further than your eyes. This way, you will spend increased time looking above your clip. The more that you can do, the better it will feel.

You can expand this exercise by clipping only at your waist, so that you always remain above your clip. Remember the breathing and pre climb psychological warm ups. The more of this you are able to do, the more you will be able to control your fear when on a route. As your confidence grows, increase the grade of the climbs you are undertaking, slowly. The combination of this and the fall training below will result in you having the confidence to climb hard moves while above your clip and not be scared of the fall. You only therefore have to concentrate on the climbing rather than the off-putting, on edge feeling most of us experience when we lead.

Lead Falls - Start Small, Get Bigger.

Note * The training plan below considers falling on indoor or manmade structures. With outdoor crags there is much more to consider to ensure you remain safe while practicing falling. With sport routes, you need to consider the quality and the safety of the bolts you will be falling on to. Prior to undertaking any falling training you should have inspected the bolts and ensured that the wall is free from features or hazards which could cause injury when you undertake the fall training. With traditional climbing, I do not advocate intentionally falling on your protection without the safety of a back up rope. If you wish to test your gear placements or practise falling while trad climbing, I recommend that advice is sought from a suitably qualified instructor.

Moving on to taking indoor lead falls, there are some training exercises which can start to build your confidence. Similar to a top rope fall, practise with a competent belayer on a vertical or slightly overhanging wall with no volumes or obvious hazards. First, only take practise falls from at least a height where you will not come close to the ground or would end up landing on the rope. This is likely to be from at least the third clip for a small fall and may be much higher if you are taking larger falls. You can start with roughly 30 cm of slack in the system and taking a controlled hop off the wall. This should result in a small fall probably of around a meter (with rope stretch). Ensure that you gain a similar balanced stance as taking the top rope falls. Take a small hop back into the seated, lower off position. To make you feel more secure you can place one hand on your knot, however take care not to hold further up the rope to avoid getting your fingers or hand trapped in the quickdraw. This has happened in the past and can cause serious injury.

Once you are happy taking small hops, you can move higher up the wall and take a slightly larger step up. Gain a balanced stance and take a slightly larger hop. Ensure that you are gaining confidence in jumping into the seated position. It is tempting in a larger fall to put your feet down to the ground. Avoid this, as you will swing into the wall and land with your toes, knees, hips, elbows, chest and / or face. None of which will be pleasant. If you find that you are putting your feet down to the floor, practise the smaller jumps again until you are able to undertake this. As your confidence grows you can take larger and larger jumps. I would recommend that the maximum slack you should jump with is the distance between clips and only when you are sufficiently high to undertake this safely. This will be a large enough fall in itself and greater falls than this do not carry any further benefit while greatly increasing the risk of an accident.

Clip Drops.

Another method of gaining confidence with falling is to practise clip drops. This is where you clip in, then without hesitation, drop off the wall. To practise this training method, clip the first three quickdraws as you normally would do. Do not undertake jumps on the first or second quickdraw to ensure that you do not land on, or get tangled with the rope or belayer when you fall. As soon as you have clipped the third quickdraw, drop off the wall. (This is why the exercise is called clip - drops). You should find that you have a small, controlled fall as the slack in the rope comes tight. Again attempt to jump into the seated position and land with your feet. The belayer should concentrate on ensuring that there is minimal slack in the system to avoid a larger fall. For the first few attempts, you may wish to pause for a few seconds to ensure that any excess slack (more than 15 cm) is taken in. Once you are caught, get back on the wall and continue to the 4th clip. Drop. Get back on the wall, climb to the 5th clip. Drop. Get back on the wall. Repeat to the top. This trains both the climber to be able to fall and the belayer to only pay out as much rope as is needed.

Once you and the belayer have gained confidence, you may wish to push a little further. Start similar to the Clip - Drop exercise. From the 3rd clip, once clipped, drop off. From the 4th clip, where you should have sufficient height (although use your own judgement) make the 4th clip, move, drop. This means after you have clipped, rather than dropping straight away, make the next move, then drop. The belayer should not take in rope if you are below the quickdraw, however should pay out enough for you to undertake the move if you are above it. You will find that making small moves will result in a moderate fall. Anywhere up to a couple of meters if you are above your clip. The advantage of making the next move before dropping off is; rather than being in a balanced position, by making a move, you are simulating making a move which has resulted in a fall. Especially if you are twisting while making the move, this can feel particularly scary to begin with because we have to drop, and twist back into having your hips parallel to the wall, then land in the seated position.

The last extension of the clip drop, is the clip, move, move drop. Similar to the above, only consider undertaking this where you are certain to fall safely, likely to be at least the 4th clip, however use your judgement. This is where you would clip, then take two moves before dropping off. Again the belayer should not be taking in, but only feeding out when you are above the clip. With two moves however it is likely that they will need to feed rope out unless you are clipping very high above your head or making very small moves. The likely circumstance is that you will climb almost up to the next clip before you drop off, resulting in a very respectable and realistic, but safe lead fall. This is much more realistic to what will be likely to happen when you are lead climbing and as a result is much more use than taking repeated, large (albeit fun) lead falls.

Unplanned Lead Falls.

In the falling section up to now, we have started to embrace falling. By the time you have reached this stage, you should be confident to take planned falls. These falls are all expected both by the climber and the belayer. Unplanned falls however, seem much more scary to us. In reality the actual fall itself is not particularly scary. By the time we realise that we have actually fallen, the rope has already caught us. The part that people find scary however is the time before the fall, desperately clinging on, fighting the dread of actually having a fall. In some cases climbers prefer to grab bigger holds to stop the fall. In others people prefer to jump off, taking a controlled fall rather than risk making another move. The majority of climbers therefore do not climb to their limits because of this reason. If you have gained the confidence to climb above your clip, control your breathing and fear and take planned lead falls, taking unplanned lead falls is your next step.

Similar to practicing top roping falls, you are likely to take lead falls as a result of two main reasons:

- Slapping for holds which you do not latch.
- As a result of tiredness and muscle failure.

These two issues have already been discussed in the top rope section and exercises provided to increase your confidence and comfort zone. Lead training for both unplanned falls and letting go as a result of muscle failure involve essentially the same exercises. In the lead variation of these exercises, for safety, only commence the exercise when you are safely clipped **at least half way up the wall**. This will be likely to involve leading an easier route until half way, then transferring to the harder route to commence the exercise at a safe height.

For working harder routes and practicing moves you might not make: Climb an easy route until half height, then transfer onto a route around your top rope limit so that you can practise repeatedly hard moves and as a consequence - falling.

Leading while pumped and not knowing whether you will make the next move or clip can be particularly scary. The only way to know how far you are able to push yourself is to climb until the point of failure. As mentioned above, ensure that you lead an easy route until at least half way up the wall before transferring onto a route which will get you tired without having to make particularly hard moves. The same as the top roped variation, continue until muscle failure, however each time you complete the route and are lowered to the floor, before you can climb again, you will need to pull the rope through. As soon as you reach the floor, get back on the wall and hang the start holds until your belayer has pulled through the rope. This will stop you from getting a rest each time you reach the floor.

When practicing these last two exercises remember that you are practicing the hardest and most hated of climbing (falling) exercises. You will also be extremely tempted to grab bigger holds or to jump off to avoid the unplanned lead fall. Avoid this urge unless the fall would be unreasonably large, unsafe or result in injury. Once you are able to control your fear, your barriers to lead climbing will have been removed and you can climb to your potential.

Coaching:

When teaching or coaching leading and undertaking fall training, some of the exercises above are too much for new or nervous lead climbers. Consider what the aim of the session is. Undertaking clip drops, or just taking a couple of controlled but large, fast lead falls, may be a quick way of introducing falling. But if the climber leaves more scared or does not get the technique right all that is risked is injury and reduced confidence. I have certainly viewed sessions where someone new to leading is effectively chucked, screaming off a route. I often wonder if this method is really a helpful part of the session? Does it really teach the climber correct falling technique, or how to land safely or is it just saving some time for the instructor?

Slowing down lead falls with the aid of an additional top rope can introduce climbers to falling while gaining confidence in falling further and training them to raise their feet and land safely. This training can be done over a number of stages (personally I use 5). Stage 1 is a slow lower onto the lead rope to see where the climber will land. Each subsequent stage gets faster until level 5 is a full speed lead fall. The advantage of this training is that the climber (and belayer) gain confidence in faster landings, and the climber can train from hop off to landing.

Climbers are tempted on larger faster falls to put their feet to the floor. If they do this, they will swing flat into the wall risking injury. Using this exercise, you will be able to monitor their falling technique with slower falls and only progress to faster falls when they are able to demonstrate a safe landing. The benefits of this are safer session delivery and a smoother learning curve for the climber.

Chapter 6 - Plateauing and Continual Improvement.

Plateauing happens to all of us. It is where we reach a certain level and remain trapped, unable to progress onto harder routes. There may be many different reasons as to why people plateau, and can be hard to overcome. Taking time to establish the cause of the plateau will enable you to train effectively and push past this barrier.

Image any sports person or physical athlete where an element of skill and technique is involved in their sport. Examples to consider could be: Ballet and Dance, Football, Hockey, Motor Sport, Golf etc. This could be anyone, however it helps if you are reasonably knowledgeable about that sport. What is the main difference between a good amateur and a professional. While many people focus on the amazing skills or tricks a professional may be able to demonstrate, is it these advanced skills or something else that separates them from amateurs? In many cases (and no doubt there are many exceptions) it boils down to a professional having a better grasp and ability to undertake the basic techniques underpinning that sport flawlessly, more consistently or quicker. For us to progress further, we should consider whether we can get more out of our technique or whether our technique remains efficient as the routes get harder.

In climbing, the differences between route difficulties is likely to be:

- Smaller or less positive holds.
- Larger moves.
- Moves which are more committing and more likely to result in a fall if not made (covered in falling section).
- More strengthy moves or more overall endurance required.

By the time you have completed the fundamentals in Set 1, moved on to twisting in Set 2 and further refined the techniques in Set 3, you should be climbing technically well. Many people plateau at this point and find that the climb differences above limit their further progress.

Smaller Holds.

To gain further technical confidence on smaller holds, there are a number of things to consider:

- Can your footwork be improved further?
- Have you practised the hand holds - Crimps?
- Does your centre of gravity (in relation to the direction of pull) need refinement as the holds get smaller?
- Are your shoes sufficient to push on smaller holds?

Having undertaken the initial exercises regarding footwork, you are likely to be able to use small footholds roughly 2-3 cm in size. You should be able to undertake each foot placement with one touch, precise footwork and no ankle bounce testing. The same principles apply to placing your feet on smaller holds. When looking at climbers moving onto smaller foot holds, is there an increase in testing the footholds? In many cases, while they have learned to place their feet well on larger holds, as the size of the holds drops down, they test more, tend to drag or bounce their feet towards the foothold and rush the placements. This is because they do not have as much faith in their footwork and counteract this by pulling harder with the arms rather than correctly rocking over their foot. As we looked at in Set 1, this is a very inefficient way to climb and should be avoided.

To gain confidence on smaller holds, practise the footwork, balance and straight arm exercises in Set 1. This should be undertaken in the same way with four weeks dedicated to each technique. By the time you are working on straight arms, your balance and footwork should have improved sufficiently to lean off straight arms.

Repeat each section relating to smaller hand holds and refining your balance point. Again, you should work on each topic for four weeks before moving on.

If, after practicing the three topics above you are still not confident at placing your feet on smaller holds lastly consider whether your shoes are up to the task? By now you should have a fair amount of experience placing your feet perfectly on the holds and rocking your weight over your feet. If your feet continue to slip consider the following factors surrounding your shoes.

- Are your shoes reasonably tight - can you easily wiggle your toes?
- How worn are your shoes?
- What type of shoe do you have?

Your first or second pair of shoes are likely to have been more for comfort rather than technical progression and it may be time to upgrade. Shoes which allow too much movement for the toes to bend back as you put weight on to the foot are likely to be too loose to use on smaller holds. If your current shoes have worn much of the rubber off the edges, they will become rounded and unable to gain suitable purchase on small holds. On the other hand, more aggressive, downturned shoes are likely to be too painful to use on slabs. For edging and moving onto smaller holds you need flat shoes which focus your weight onto the toe. They should be tight, giving partial toe crimp, but nothing too dramatic as this will just be painful. Having shoes with fairly stiff rubber will provide more support on smaller holds, but the trade-off is that you can feel less. Aim for something which will provide a good deal of support and feel. At this stage, you may wish to look for all round shoes which will perform well on most varieties of wall, and if needed invest in specific, more aggressive shoes for seriously overhanging climbs when you need that little bit more. It is pointless however buying shoes which are not designed for your climbing style. Just because your climbing hero has aggressive, downturned shoes for overhanging climbs, if you are mainly climbing slabs, having the same shoes won't lend to you rocking over your feet.

Larger Moves.

Large moves cause most people difficulty. How many times have you heard or said - "I have good technique, but I am too short"? Granted if you are standing on the only hold on a slab, and the next hold is out of reach, that route may be a bit too reachy for you. How many times does this happen though? Our main problem is not on slabs, it is on vertical and overhanging walls where we cannot reach as far. People almost always equate a lack of reach for a lack of strength. "I can't pull to the next hold!" Think how far you can pull. Many of us can hang off a hold. Most can pull up until our arms are bent at 90 degrees, some of us can pull until our chin is by the hold. However all of this only gives us an arms length to the next hold. Simulate this in front of a mirror. You can see how little is achieved by pulling compared to the exertion required to make the move. Twisting on the other hand keeps us balanced and stable while hanging on a straight arm. To make larger moves, we need to get more comfortable getting our feet higher and exaggerating our twist so that our holding hand can get lower resulting in a further reach. This has been covered in exaggerated twisting. Further practise can result in you being able to reach almost 2 arm lengths and is therefore vitally important to progress. If this reach issue is causing your failure to progress, undertake 8 weeks of making larger moves. Start on large holds which are easy to use and slowly drop down the size of the holds while making larger and larger moves. It may be needed to make up new routes or problems to your training requirements but practise making these move types until your confidence increases.

Chapter 7 - The Training Plan.

Prior to undertaking any part of this training plan, ensure that you use the normal warm up you would undertake before any climbing session.

For all of the following exercise training sets firstly refresh yourself of the initial sections and the exercises. Undertake this on the first week of each set. Following this, you should climb an easy route trying to perfect the skill you are working on. Your training partner should focus on the skill that you are practising and count the number of mistakes you make during the course of the climb. When you have finished the climb make a note of the number of mistakes made and the reasons behind the score. An example is footwork: 3 for testing, 4 for repositioning the foot and 2 for not looking. This will provide you with some focus to reduce these errors during the upcoming weeks.

On each training session (in addition to the initial exercises on week 1), you should climb 7-10 routes or 21 - 30 boulder problems focusing only on the one aspect of your climbing you are training. You should start with very easy climbs and commence each session with the same grade each week. Your aim should not be to get to the top, but to execute each technique perfectly. Your belayer will need to assist you. Their role will be to provide you feedback on your climbing and tell you when you make mistakes and what the mistake was. When a mistake is made, your belayer takes away a life. Each session, you have a reduced amount of lives per climb, indicated on the weekly plan. When you lose all your lives, you have to return to the floor and climb the same route again. If you reach the top with lives left, you should move onto a more difficult climb. You should only increase the difficulty by a maximum of one grade at a time. Note the maximum grade completed on each session.

At the end of each block of training undertake an evaluation. Consider your skill level at the start and award yourself a score for your initial confidence. Score yourself 1 - 10 with 1 being the lowest and 10 being the highest. Award yourself a second score of 1-10, this should be your confidence in the skill after the completion of the training module. You should be able to chart your perceived improvement over the weeks. You can also consider how many mistakes you made on the initial route where your partner made note of all the mistakes you made. Consider what grade you are now able to climb with less errors. Both ways are effective of demonstrating your progress.

Your belayer should also take a few minutes independently to consider the skill you have been working on. They should consider what has improved. Whether there is any further improvement required and also provide you a score between 1 - 10. You should be able to chart improvement both via the grades climbed, but also how the technique looks compared to the example videos provided. Videos of the first and last week can also provide good feedback.

After you have undertaken each technique in the Set, you should spend another 4 weeks putting all the aspects together. You should complete the Set evaluation tasks and scores which will determine whether you should complete specific parts or the whole section again. If you are confident in the techniques in that Set, you can move on to the next.

Set 1 - The Fundamentals.

Straight Arms.

Straight arms perfects efficiency and reducing your need on physical upper body strength. This should all be undertaken on a vertical wall.

You will lose a life for making the following errors:

- Bending the arm you are holding on with.
- Using handholds in the wrong direction of pull.

Week	Lives per climb	------------------------------------	Hardest Vertical Grade Achieved
1	Initial Straight Arm Exercises 5 lives	Number of mistakes on initial climb:	
2	4 lives	----------------------------------	
3	3 Lives	----------------------------------	
4	2 Lives	----------------------------------	
Evaluation	Initial confidence (1-10)	End Confidence (1-10)	Further improvement
Belayer evaluation	What has improved?	What needs further improvement?	Overall (1-10)

Good Balance.

Good balance reduces weight from the arms and focuses it onto the feet, making placements feel safer and less likely to fail / slip. You should climb on a variety of slabs and vertical walls.

You will lose a life for making the following errors:

- On the slab - failing to sufficiently rock the Centre of Gravity over the foot:
    - Unable to remove lower foot from the hold.
    - Having to pull with the hands.
    - Reaching the balance point and returning to an off balanced position prior to pushing.
- On a Vertical Wall
    - Not leaning off handholds the correct way.
    - Reaching the hands outside of the feet.
    - Not considering Centre of Gravity prior to each move.

Week	Lives per climb	Hardest Slab Grade	Hardest Vertical Grade
1	Initial Balance Exercises 5 Lives	Number of mistakes made on initial climb:	
2	4 Lives		
3	3 Lives		
4	2 Lifes		
Evaluation	Initial confidence (1-10)	End Confidence (1-10)	Further improvement
Belayer evaluation	What has improved?	What needs further improvement?	Overall (1-10)

Precise Footwork.

Footwork will perfect precision and trust. This can be undertaken on a slab or a vertical wall.

You will lose a life for making the following errors:

- Incorrect part of the foot on the hold – tip toes, ball of the foot, the arch or outside edge.
- Not looking at the foot hold / scraping the foot up the wall to get to the hold.
- Imprecise placement where there is not as much contact between foot and hold as possible.
- Repositioning the foot without removing it and replacing it again.
- Testing or Ankle bouncing. If foot is removed and replaced, this can be allowed.

Week	Lives per climb	Hardest Slab Grade	Hardest Vertical Grade
1	Initial Footwork Exercises: 5 Lives	Number of mistakes on initial climb:	
2	4 Lives		
3	3 Lives		
4	2 Lives		
Evaluation	Initial confidence (1-10)	End Confidence (1-10)	Further improvement
Belayer evaluation	What has improved?	What needs further improvement?	Overall (1-10)

Set 2 Introducing Twisting - The Outside Edge.

The introducing twisting section lasts 8 weeks and by the end of it you should be proficient at using the outside edge twist. For all future training sessions, in addition to your usual warm up, you should climb a slab twice and a vertical wall twice to continue to improve the skills learned in Set 1. Following this, undertake a section of a traverse wall - up to 10 moves three times. The traverse should focus on twisting and correctly using the outside edge. Following the traverse, move onto vertical and overhanging walls. Overhangs should not be attempted until at least week 4 to enable you to have reasonable proficiency in the technique before the difficulty increases.

You will lose a life for making the following common errors:

- Bending the arm you are holding on with.
- Pulling with the arms
- Twisting the wrong way.
- Getting the arms and legs out of sync.
- Positioning your feet too high or too wide.
- Hips not twisting enough - they should be close to the wall.

Week	Lives per climb	Hardest Vertical Grade	Hardest Overhang Grade
1	Initial Outside Edge Exercises		-----------------------------------
2	5 Lives		-----------------------------------
3	5 Lives		-----------------------------------
4	4 Lives		
5	4 Lives		
6	4 Lives		
7	3 Lives		
8	1 Live		
Evaluation	Initial confidence (1-10)	End Confidence (1-10)	Further improvement
Belayer evaluation	What has improved?	What needs further improvement?	Overall (1-10)

Set 2: Introducing Flagging

To introduce Flagging repeat this section for another 4 weeks. This time, **where a flag is more efficient than swapping feet** and using the outside edge, introduce this into the section. For the first week you should practise flagging, then continue climbing a variety of vertical walls and overhangs introducing this technique when needed.

Week	Lives per climb	Hardest Vertical Grade	Hardest Overhang Grade
1	Initial Flag Exercises	Learning to flag, Recap of Outside edge movement.	
2	5 Lives		
3	4 Lives		
4	3 Lives		
Evaluation	Initial confidence (1-10)	End Confidence (1-10)	Further improvement
Belayer evaluation	What has improved?	What needs further improvement?	Overall (1-10)

Set 3 - Further efficiency skills.

Pivoting and Drop Knees.

Pivoting is a further extension of twisting. You should only attempt to introduce this skill when you have a comprehensive knowledge of using the outside edge and flagging and you are climbing routes back up to your previous limit without making mistakes. You should undertake 4 weeks of practise pivoting with one foot before moving onto pivoting with both feet. You should undertake the pivoting with either or both feet for a further 4weeks. Many of the climbers I regularly coach incorporate a traverse into their warm up, practicing pivoting with both feet long after the skill has been learned. This ensures they continue to climb efficiently and utilise this technique as their favoured way of climbing.

Week	Lives per climb	Hardest Vertical Grade	Hardest Overhang Grade
1	Initial Pivot Exercises 5 Lives	Effective use of pivoting.	
2	5 Lives		
3	4 Lives		
4	4 Lives		
5	3 Lives		
6	2 Lives		
7	2 Lives		
8	1 Lives		
Evaluation	Initial confidence (1-10)	End Confidence (1-10)	Further improvement
Belayer evaluation	What has improved?	What needs further improvement?	Overall (1-10)

Further Training Efficiencies.

You should now be introducing small drop knees and movement on an overhang should be fairly efficient only needing small refinement. A further extension of this is to raise the feet and produce exaggerated drop knees. This can be undertaken for another 4 weeks as required.

The following further efficiency skills can be introduced on a need to know basis. Again, you should practise them for a number of weeks until you are satisfied that you are executing the skills correctly:

- Bouldering Sit Starts
- Exaggerated Twisting - Big Moves
- Bridging, Palming and Planting
- Heel / Toe Hooks
- Dynamic Moves (likely to require 8 weeks.)

A blank training plan in included below for you complete to your needs.

Week	Lives	Wall type 1	Wall type 2
1	5 Lives		
2	4 Lives		
3	3 Lives		
4	2 Lives		
Evaluation	Initial confidence (1-10)	End Confidence (1-10)	Further improvement
Belayer evaluation	What has improved?	What needs further improvement?	Overall (1-10)

Falling / Fear Training.

Dealing with fear will be improved differently to the other improvement plans. You should complete the comfort zone table included below. Things you are very confident with should be placed into the green area. Things you are able to undertake, but you find scary should be placed into the orange area. Things you are too scared to attempt are placed into the red section. There is a completed example of this table in the falling section. You may need to tailor the table to suit your needs. For example, you may be very confident at bouldering and top rope with no elements of your climbing in the orange or red zones. On the other hand, most of the aspects of lead climbing are in the orange and red areas. It is common to have a certain area of your climbing which seems more scary others.

Order the aspects from least to most scary and start to train the aspects in the orange zone. There are various examples of how to train each area considered in the dealing with fear section. Monitor regularly how you are progressing with the aspect you are training. Once your comfort zone expands so that the aspect has moved into the green zone, train the next aspect on the list. This progression will gradually expand your comfort zone and given time will enable you to conquer your climbing fears.

If you are able to climb three times per week, you can undertake the falling / fear training on a differing night per week from the technique training. If you are only able to climb twice per week you should undertake falling or technical improvement. This way you still have a session dedicated to rewarding, fun climbing without all of your climbing sessions focusing on performance increases.

It is likely to take many months if not years to become completely comfortable with falling. It is one of the most important things which you will do however and is worth taking the time to train.

Comfort Zone Table -

Boulder	Top Rope	Lead

Conclusion.

Thank you for purchasing this book. I hope that it has been both (slightly) enjoyable and helpful to your climbing and / or provided you with some ideas on how to effectively coach aspiring climbers. I would love to hear how you have progressed and if you are climbing harder as a result, so please leave us a post or message us on the Plastic Heroes Climbing Shop Facebook page. If you have any specific questions regarding your training, please email or message me and I will do my best to answer your enquiry.

List Of Thanks.

The Reach Climbing Wall for allowing us to use the facilities to prepare the photos and videos.

https://thereach.org.uk/

Vaidotas Monstavicius for filming and editing the videos.

Www.vclimbing.wordpress.com

Www.thebigones.net

Pascale Michalski for editing the photos.

https://www.facebook.com/redpoint.painting/

Many of the photos and videos included in this book are of climbers who volunteered to assist in this project. The videos were filmed firstly with no coaching, then repeated after a few minutes of explanation and practise. I wish to thank the volunteers for attending the sessions and for allowing their videos to be used in this book.

The proof readers for correcting my just terrible spelling and grammar.

Cassie, for everything.

Contact Details:

http://plasticheroes.co.uk/perfect-technique-for-climbers-book-resource-page/

Paul Barr – paulbarr80@hotmail.com